Y0-DWO-777
CHICAGO
HAROLD WASHINGTON LIBRARY
R0014741870

Research in Teacher Education

A SYMPOSIUM

CONTRIBUTORS

S. C. T. Clarke, *University of Alberta*

Norma Furst, *Temple University*

M. Ray Loree, *University of Alabama*

Frederick J. McDonald, *Educational Testing Services, Princeton, N. J.*

Robert F. Peck, *University of Texas*

Barak Rosenshine, *University of Illinois*

Richard L. Turner, *Indiana University*

Research in Teacher Education

A SYMPOSIUM

Edited by

B. OTHANEL SMITH

University of South Florida

for the American Educational Research Association

PRENTICE-HALL, INC., *Englewood Cliffs, N.J.*

13-774455-2

Library of Congress Catalog Card Number: 73-138471

Current printing (last digit):

10 9 8 7 6 5 4 3 2 1

PRENTICE-HALL INTERNATIONAL, INC., *London*
PRENTICE-HALL OF AUSTRALIA PTY. LTD., *Sydney*
PRENTICE-HALL OF CANADA LTD., *Toronto*
PRENTICE-HALL OF INDIA PRIVATE LIMITED, *New Delhi*
PRENTICE-HALL OF JAPAN, INC., *Tokyo*

Printed in the United States of America

Contents

Research in Teacher Education

A SYMPOSIUM

1

Introduction

B. OTHANEL SMITH

Were it not for the fact that about one thousand higher institutions are producing 200,000 beginning teachers per year, there would be little point to this symposium, for the chief purpose of research on the education of teachers is to improve the programs of teacher preparation in these institutions. These programs have developed over the last hundred years, and especially since the beginning of the present century, on the basis of meager and inadequate knowledge acquired largely from the practical experience of teachers, general psychological principles, and studies in philosophy and the social sciences. The problem which confronts those who are concerned with research on teacher education involves a quest for more dependable knowledge of teaching behavior—its elements and their influence on pupil learning. But even if there were an abundance of such knowledge, there would still be the problems of training teachers to use it in their practice and of inducing institutional changes that incorporate these training procedures into preparatory programs—a task comparable to rebuilding vehicles while they are in motion.

It is barely four decades since the first empirical studies of teacher education were made, if we count the studies of Barr (1929) as the beginning. Since that time a large number of such studies have been made. How many is anyone's guess, but enough to fill a handbook of research on teaching and to justify a revision of it. Yet we keep asking ourselves how much dependable knowledge do we have with which to build more effective programs of teacher education? Some critics, viewing the mountain of data interpreted by statistical techniques—standard deviations, coefficients of correlation, regression equations, and what have you—exclaim that there is less here than meets the eye. This may be true. But if so, it is no reason for pessimism, for every item of hard knowledge springs out of a slush pile of data and interpretations heaped up by adventures that left the main questions unanswered.

What is research on teacher education? In a sense this question is naïve, for everyone must know already what teacher education is, and that research on it is simply the systematic study of problems that arise in the course of carrying it on. Generally speaking, research on teacher education attempts to answer the question of how the behavior of an individual in preparation for teaching can be made to conform to acceptable patterns. But if we are to come closer to the concrete realities of what research on teacher education is about, it is necessary to mention the main areas of such education and then to indicate the sorts of problem that arise in each of them.

Specifically, then, any adequate program of teacher education provides for (1) training in skills, (2) teaching of pedagogical concepts and principles, (3) developing relevant attitudes, and (4) teaching the various subject matters of instruction. The first three of these have long been considered professional preparation while the last one has been counted as academic or nonprofessional. These labels have become questionable in recent years, and today the tendency is to consider the academic work of the teacher as part of his professional preparation insofar as it is adapted to the requirements of teaching. However, in this symposium only the first three are discussed.

The question of how skills of teaching are to be developed has long confronted the teacher educator. The commonsense way of approaching this problem has been to follow the apprentice pattern used in the teaching of various arts and crafts. Sometimes this approach to training has been reduced to short periods of apprentice teaching under the supervision of teachers whose skills were little better than those of the persons they were training. In other cases, the teacher-in-training has been assigned to a teacher of higher quality. It was supposed that, by observing and studying the performance of the critic teacher and by practicing under his supervision, the teacher-in-training would acquire the skills appropriate for effective classroom work.

This way of developing teaching skills has been criticized from many different standpoints during the past quarter of a century, but no thorough evaluation of the system of practice teaching has been made. Any thorough review of studies of the effects of practice teaching on attitudes or on the skills of teaching ends in a quandary. Practice teaching is now in the process of being replaced, or seriously modified, not because it has been conclusively shown to be ineffective but because more promising modes of teacher training have now become possible.

A major breakthrough in the training of teachers occurred when teaching behavior was conceived to be a complex of skills that could be identified and practiced systematically under specifiable conditions (McDonald and Allen, 1967). This conception probably arose from advancements in technological devices for recording and reproducing behavior. The teacher-in-training can now observe and analyze his performance of a particular skill as his behavior is played back. In subsequent practices he can modify his performances in indicated ways and thus improve it with practice.

Along with this breakthrough came a new emphasis in the analysis of teaching behavior. Almost from ancient times it has been assumed that the way teachers should behave in the classroom could be derived from what philosophers, and in recent decades psychologists, said about thinking and learning. In this view, teaching behavior is believed to be conventional, and therefore laden with the misconceptions and practices inherited from centuries of trial and error. Accordingly, improvement in teaching is to be brought about by replacing these conventional behaviors with behaviors derived from learning theory and philosophical conceptions of thinking. While this approach to the formulation of teaching skills has not been abandoned, it has been challenged as an exclusive approach by research workers who conceive of teaching behavior as worthy of study in its own right. Some of these workers assume that teaching behavior is as natural as economic or political behavior, and all of them believe that its components must first be understood before it can be improved by the use of psychological knowledge.

These two points of view—that teaching behavior should be analyzed in terms of the psychology of learning, and that it should be studied in its own right—are not contradictory, as is often claimed, but complementary. Teaching behavior no doubt incorporates elements that can be improved, and their improvement can doubtless be effected by studying them in the light of psychological knowledge. For example, teaching behavior naturally includes acts of approval and disapproval, and reinforcement theory makes it possible to improve this aspect of the behavior. Nevertheless, the various conceptions of teaching have given rise to theoretical controversies, which in turn pose the question of how teaching is to be conceptualized for research purposes.

All sorts of dissections of teaching behavior have been made since the closing years of the 1940s (Simon and Boyer, 1967). We have witnessed the analysis of teaching behavior into emotional, cognitive, and other psychological categories as well as into logical, pedagogical, linguistic, and social categories. It is not easy to tell which of these various classes of behavior are actually different from one another and which are different only in name. We can decide on conceptual grounds that the affective categories are different from the cognitive categories. But formulations of each of these two genera are so vague and ambiguous as to make empirical differentiations between them difficult except in extreme cases. Despite all of our efforts, we apparently have no generally accepted conceptual system, psychological or otherwise, by which either to formulate or to identify the skills of teaching. Fortunately, the lack of such a system does not preclude research. We can and do go ahead with the job of formulating, identifying, and testing out various skills and other aspects of teaching behavior as the winds of doctrine blow about us. On the other hand, it is clear that research would be advanced measurably by a conceptual system for formulating and identifying teaching skill. There is need, therefore, for continuous efforts to handle the problem of conceptualization, for by digging deeper into the structure of teaching, we may find more powerful variables. The issues that swirl about the task of conceptualizing teaching are explored in Chapter 2.

No matter how effective training procedures may be or how fruitful conceptions of learning or teaching may be in generating ways of conducting instruction, teaching will not be improved if the skills taught in teacher education programs have no greater influence upon pupil learning than the skills teachers ordinarily use. To resort to an analogy, there would be no point in teaching the farmer to change his practices if the new practices increase the productivity of the land by zero amount. To establish skills of higher yield, research workers have conducted studies to determine the effects of various types of teaching behavior upon pupils. In pursuit of such skills some research workers have conducted laboratory studies of meaningful learning. Others have studied the effect of procedures used in various subject matter areas either under classroom conditions or in laboratory situations. Other workers have conducted experimental classroom studies in which the effects of variations in teaching procedures are ascertained. And still others have made correlational studies in which teaching behaviors are related to measures of pupil growth. All of these studies are critically reviewed in Chapter 3 for the purpose of answering the question of whether or not there are teaching behaviors so closely related to pupil growth that they can be justifiably included in programs of teacher education.

From the tough-minded analysis set forth in Chapter 3 we are forced to conclude that there are few, if any, skills of teaching whose superiority can be counted as empirically established. All approaches, except correlational studies, have yielded knowledge of little worth to teacher education. And even correlational studies give only rough approximations to efficacious teaching behaviors. In these studies only high inference-level variables, such as clarity and enthusiasm, yield significant correlations with measures of pupil growth. But these sorts of variables yield little if any content or specific skills for a teacher education program. They tell little if anything about what to train a teacher to do in order to be clear or enthusiastic. Until these highly abstract variables are analyzed into specific behaviors, they can be of little use to the teacher educator.

Perhaps the most stimulating parts of Chapter 3 are the suggestions for designing correlational studies, analyzing the results, and selecting variables. It is apparent from this chapter that the primary value of high inference-level variables is not their usefulness to the teacher educator, but the direction which they give to further research. Beginning with such concepts as clarity, the research worker can begin to explore the variables analytically, in the hope of reducing them to elements that can be used in programs of teacher education without the loss of their empirical grounding. Unfortunately for some high-inference concepts, this hope may turn out to be forlorn.

Teacher education can hardly be separated from notions about how pupils learn; what teachers are taught to believe and do and how they are taught almost inevitably will be shaped by ideas of the process of learning. Hence, since students appear to learn in various ways, it is not strange that there are different conceptions of teacher preparation, or that research on teacher education may be, and often is, controlled by different points of view. In one of the most generally accepted perspectives, teaching is seen in terms of skills and concepts useful in teaching any and all normal pupils with a minimum of adjustment to individuals. This perspective emphasizes the teacher as a controlling figure and the pupils as the recipients of his instruction.

In opposition to this perspective is the view that the pupil can be taught to carry on the learning process himself, to be self-directing, in a measure to teach himself. In order for teachers to produce pupils of this degree of self-control and self-instruction, it appears that skills different from those in the teacher-controlled perspective are indicated. What these skills are and how they may be taught is the subject of Chapter 4. Here the reader will find a defense of individualized teaching as an effective way of helping pupils acquire coping behavior, and a stimulating discussion of how teachers can be trained to use the appropriate concepts and skills. In Chapter 5 the same view of teaching is explored theoretically. The author of this chapter claims that this form of teaching, like the teacher-controlled form, requires the pupil to decode, transform, memorize, retrieve, and encode. In addition, however, it requires that rules and procedures for searching and a disposition to search be engendered by the teacher. But basically, it is argued, there is no difference between the two approaches except in regard to what they are used for. Thus the conventional distinctions between heuristics and didactics appear to be questionable on theoretical grounds.

Turning now to the preparation of the teacher in pedagogical theory, it is clear that teachers not only engage, either skillfully or unskillfully, in interactions with their pupils, but that they also interpret pupil behavior. Interviews with experienced teachers indicate that the concepts they use to interpret pupil behavior are simple and include few elements of the sophisticated knowledge found in studies of educational psychology (Jackson, 1968). This fact bears out the long line of preservice teachers who have claimed that educational psychology, educational sociology, educational philosophy, and other theoretical courses are unrelated to the classroom work they are called upon to do as student-teachers.

The failure of teachers to make use of the sophisticated concepts and principles found in pedagogical studies hase been explained in a number of ways. Some students of education maintain that the rate and density of events that occur in an ordinary classroom are so high that a teacher simply cannot view these events in fundamental ways and still maintain the interactive process with his pupils (Jackson, 1968). On the other hand, these same observers claim there is some reason to suppose that experienced teachers do make use of many theoretical ideas when they are reflecting upon their work before and after class sessions. Other students, however, hold the view that perhaps the more sophisticated knowledge is not used because such knowledge is not taught in a meaningful context. The current practice is to teach concepts from a textbook by elaborating upon them in abstraction and illustrating them by verbal examples.

When we reflect upon the fact that the preservice teacher typically devotes half of his pedagogical studies to theoretical materials, it is peculiar that so little research has been done to find out the utility of theoretical knowledge in the teacher's work. Perhaps the paucity of such research can be attributed to the belief that differences in teacher effectiveness can be reduced to differences in attitudes and skills, and that concepts make no difference save as they influence these elements of behavior. Furthermore, the sorts of skills and attitudes that research workers have been concerned with tend to be those which are perhaps more easily associated with the simple concepts of the teacher than with the sophisticated ones of theoretical pedagogy. But whatever the proper explanation may be, the utility of pedagogical knowledge should be thoroughly explored empirically.

One approach is to consider that the utility of conceptual knowledge lies in the interpretation of behavior, rather than in the improvement of skills. This sort of utility can be tested by identifying and teaching concepts which are believed to be useful in a meaningful context. It is now possible with the aid of educational technology to teach these concepts in the context of the process of interpreting what goes on in the classroom as depicted by videotapes of actual classroom interaction.

One of the most promising studies of this sort is the pilot study carried on by the Canterbury Teaching Research Project Staff, Canterbury University, New Zealand (Wright, Nuthall, and Lawrence, 1970). The study consists of three phases. The first phase attempts to find out some of the factors that influence how student-teachers perceive observed lessons. The purpose of the second phase is to learn whether or not second-year students in education can be taught in a limited time some of the basic elements of the more complex interaction analyses such as those developed by Taba (1966) and Bellack (1966). In a third phase an attempt is made to study the feasibility of using microteaching situations to shape the verbal behavior of student-teachers in the classroom. These phases are all variations of a single theme—namely, the search for ways of raising the teacher's understanding and verbal behavior above the commonsense level where it now appears to be lodged.

The research workers in this investigation make no flat claim as to its outcomes, for the study is, after all, merely exploratory. Nevertheless, it is interesting to note that their exploratory studies led them to make the following comments:

> The microteachers advanced considerably in their ability to conceptualize their own and other teaching behavior and this might provide for them their greatest long-term gain. This led them towards an increasing facility in stating specific objectives, predetermining teacher strategy congruent with these, and evaluating their teaching towards such objectives. It seemed that their teaching showed a more business-like approach and a growing economy of presentation. There was a noticeable shift of concern from content to teaching strategy [Wright, Nuthall, and Lawrence, 1970].

Perhaps the time has come when those who are engaged in research in teacher education should take more seriously the problems of determining how the theoretical knowledge of pedagogy can be rendered more effective in controlling the behavior of teachers both in the classroom and in their pre- and post-classroom activities.

When this symposium was planned, no provision was made for a discussion of the issues having to do with the utility of theoretical pedagogical knowledge. This was due not to an oversight but to the belief that the matter had not been explored thoroughly enough to justify a major paper on it. As a consequence, very little is said in this symposium about this component of the teacher's preparation. As preparation for the symposium developed, and especially after the symposium was over, it became clear to the chairman that a serious error had been made by not including a paper on this important matter.

One constantly hears the claim that personality is a factor in teaching behavior. It can be said with considerable confidence that the major line of division among research workers in the area of teacher education runs between the roles they envisage for personality and cognition in teaching. One view holds that teaching behavior is so much an expression of the teacher's personality that the skills he will use, how he will use them, and their effects on pupils' achievement are in large measure dependent upon his personality. While not rejecting the claim that personality influences teaching behavior, another view nevertheless holds that research in teacher education has been so preoccupied with the role of personality, and the affective aspects of behavior it entails, that the cognitive dimension of teaching behavior has been slighted.

Part of this controversy undoubtedly rests in the way the term "personality" is used. In some cases it is used to refer to the totality of a person's behavior.

When it is defined in this way, there can be little controversy over the claim that personality is a major factor in teaching, because the affective and cognitive dimensions of behavior are both included in it. In other cases, the term is used to refer to such characteristics as being withdrawn or outgoing, enthusiastic or apathetic. In still other cases, "personality" is used to designate a frame of reference with which one thinks about himself—his adequacy, worth, capacity, guilt feelings, and so forth.

The use of the term "personality" as an inclusive category of behavior is being discarded in the field of psychology and in teacher education. The tendency now is to think in terms of attitudes. Consequently, research on teaching is becoming more concerned with the problem of determining the effects of the teacher's attitudes on what he does in the classroom and on the achievement of his pupils. There can be little doubt that the attitudes a teacher has toward himself influence his behavior in the classroom. And there are strong reasons for believing that the teacher's attitudes toward his pupils—e.g., his expectations of them—will influence their achievement. There can be no doubt that personality in the attitudinal sense is a factor in teaching behavior. The question is what elements of personality make a difference in such behavior, and how these elements can be modified in directions that increase pupil growth. This question is dealt with in Chapter 6 in such a way as to suggest the different approaches to the problem of shaping the attitudes of teachers in programs of teacher education.

However meager our knowledge of teaching and the training of teachers may be, there are good reasons to believe that even such knowledge as we have is being used far too little in programs of teacher education. This belief has led many institutions, including the United States Office of Education, to become concerned with the task of designing new programs. Models for teacher education are being advanced in a number of institutions. These are models in the sense of blueprints for programs of preparation, and not models in the sophisticated theoretical and mathematical sense.

Based on an analysis of a number of designs for teacher education, and especially the Model Elementary Teacher Education Projects sponsored by the United States Office of Education, Chapter 7 presents a framework of concepts with which to analyze and think about designs for programs of teacher education. This chapter not only gives the salient features of the models but also affords a perspective from which to view the old as well as the new programs and suggests areas for developmental research.

REFERENCES

Barr, A. S., 1929. *Characteristic Differences in the Teaching Performance of Good and Poor Teachers of the Social Studies.* Bloomington, Ill.: Public School Publishing Co.

Bellack, Arno, A. Kliebard, Ronald T. Hyman, and Frank L. Smith, 1966. *The Language of the Classroom*. New York: Teachers College Press.

Jackson, Philip W., 1968. *Life in Classrooms*. New York: Holt, Rinehart and Winston, Inc.

McDonald, Frederick J., and Dwight W. Allen, 1967. *Training Effects of Feedback and Modeling Procedures on Teaching Performance*. Palo Alto, California: Stanford University Press.

Simon, Anita, and E. Gil Boyer, 1967. *Mirrors for Behavior, An Anthology of Observation Instruments*. Philadelphia: Research for Better Schools (A Regional Educational Laboratory).

Taba, Hilda, 1966. *Teaching Strategies and Cognitive Functioning in Elementary School Children*. Cooperative Research Project No. 2404. San Francisco State College

Wright, C. J., G. A. Nuthall, and P. J. Lawrence, 1970. "A Study of Classroom Interaction in the Training of Teachers," *Educational Research Newsletter*. Christ Church, New Zealand: Department of Education, University of Canterbury.

2

Conceptual Foundations of Research in Teacher Education

RICHARD L. TURNER

The point of preservice teacher education is to produce a social advantage or a savings. The advantage or savings may be counted against criteria drawn from different disciplinary perspectives. *Psychologically,* the savings should appear at the time a teacher first begins to teach. The teacher prepared in a preservice program should show greater performance proficiency on the variety of tasks that teachers ought to be able to perform than should alternatively trained teachers. Moreover, because he hypothetically starts with a learning advantage, he should increase in proficiency in his performance of very complex teaching tasks and processes more rapidly that his differently trained counterpart. *Economically,* a preservice teacher education program should reduce the cost of on-the-job training for the preservice trained person as compared to the differently trained person, assuming that the performance criteria are equivalent for both groups. *Socially* and *economically,* the preservice teacher education programs should lead to greater teacher productivity of desirable pupil behaviors than alternative programs so that, if the costs of the programs are equivalent, the unit costs of behavior production are lower among the trained teachers.

From a research viewpoint, not all of these broad criteria are equally useful in teacher education. First, economic and social criteria are in some degree associated with psychological criteria, but are more remote from training. Second, under current research methods, one would have a difficult time pinpointing the effects of particular teacher education programs among the over-all statistical outcomes resulting from large-scale economic or sociological studies of educational productivity. If research findings are to be of value in teacher education, they must at least be able to show differences between particular kinds of teacher education programs. Indeed, if research is really to be of value, it must ultimately be able to show relationships between particular treatments in particular education programs and subsequent teacher performance.

Such a requirement is a very difficult one to meet. In one sense it is impossible. One may doubt, for example, that we shall see the time when antecedent-consequent or "causal" relationships between particular aspects of a teacher education program—say a particular unit in educational psychology—and some aspect of subsequent teacher performance can be shown. The demonstration of "causal" relationships requires true experimental designs, and too many variables intervene in the process of teacher education between the treatment and the performance for anything finer than gross quasi-experimental studies to occur. That one might conduct a true experiment in some segment of a teacher education program involving a specific treatment and a specific change in behavior is of course possible. But this is a different thing from showing a causal relationship between the same treatment and a performance occurring months or years later.

The research situation confronted in teacher education is more like that confronted in economics, less like that in experimental psychology. The kind of research cycle to which we may look forward is: theory—multivariate research—arguments about causality. In studies concerning the outcomes of teacher education, this cycle is best entered into with some attention to theoretical considerations, for unless one starts with some notion of the domains of criterion variables, he is apt to have no basis for predicting such variables.

To locate the domains within which the criterion variables fall, it is useful to view teaching along three primary dimensions: structure, style, and substance. The *structure* of teaching may be described by two types of propositions: (1) those which state the logically necessary conditions which must occur in order for teaching to occur—i.e., analytic propositions about teaching; and (2) those which state the empirical conditions which must be met if teaching is to eventuate in learning—i.e., synthetic propositions about learning under conditions of teaching. These two types of propositions are logically independent. Teaching may occur without learning and learning may occur without teaching. They are not, however, valuationally independent. Teaching is valued when it eventuates in learning and not otherwise. That is why we spend so much time worrying about teacher effectiveness.

Style in teaching is wholly a matter of synthetic propositions. Propositions about style deal with variations in the way in which the operations involved in teaching are performed. To assert that certain operations must be performed in order for teaching to occur, and to assert that the performance of certain operations increases the probability that teaching will eventuate in learning, is to make assertions about the structure of teaching, but to say how variation in performance of these operations bears on the learning outcomes is to make a statement about teaching style. From a research viewpoint, statements about teaching style should be separated into two groups: those that bear on variations in specific teaching operations with individuals or groups ("task-relevant style"), and those that bear on the general mode of teacher operation in group instruction (leadership style).

Substance in teaching is on the one hand apparent and on the other obscure. One must teach *something*. In this sense, substance is a necessary condition of teaching, but it is not an operation. It is what one operates with or on. But because the amount of variation in what may be taught surely approaches infinity, substance must also be considered one of the variates in teaching which may be hypothesized to interact with style and perhaps with the synthetic aspects of structure. In the present paper, the substance of teaching receives largely incidental treatment while the focus is on matters of structure and style.

THE CRITERION PROBLEM: STRUCTURE, STYLE, AND SUBSTANCE

Structure

The analytic or logically necessary attributes of teaching are few. First, all teaching is dyadic—i.e., involves reciprocal, interdependent responding between at least two persons. That one of these persons holds the greater authority and has control of substantial reinforcements which can be delivered to or withheld from the other are common features of teaching. This dyadic quality probably should be regarded as a synthetic or empirical attribute, not an analytic attribute. Second, there must be a gap between the performance of one of the persons, the pupil, and a performance standard held by the other person, the teacher. Whether an advantage results from the student also holding the performance standard is an interesting empirical question. Third, the person holding the performance standard must engage in an hypothesized instrumentality to close the gap between the performance of the pupil and the performance standard. To assert that the teacher engages in an "hypothesized instrumentality" means that he selects a response or set of responses which he implicitly or explicitly predicts will close the gap. Sometimes this prediction is true and sometimes it is not. When it is true, teaching eventuates in learning; when it is false, no "instrumentality," no goal achieving response, has been performed, and the specific teaching act turns out to be a thing of no value.

The foregoing definition of teaching owes an intellectual debt to A. P.

Colladarci (1959), D. G. Ryans (1960), B. O. Smith (1961), and L. M. Stolurow (1965), all of whom have addressed themselves to one or another of its aspects.

The criterial synthetic attributes of teaching, the empirical conditions required for teaching to eventuate in learning, are of course debatable. At present, however, Stolurow's *Socrates* model may be taken as a reasonable statement of the conditions or operations involved in teaching under a tutorial arrangement such as that in programmed instruction or computer assisted instruction. Some modification of the model is required to make it reasonably congruent to classroom instruction.

The *Socrates* model is well known and easily accessible, so there is no point in reproducing it in the original here. What is relevant are the teaching operations suggested by the model.[1] These operations fall into two broad groups, a pretutorial group and a tutorial group. The pretutorial group contains two subgroups, *input* operations and *search and evaluation* operations. Two contiguous sets of operations fall in the input subgroup. One set requires an operation to identify the entry performance of the student, with the collateral or supplementary operations of identifying relevant aptitude and personality variates. The other set requires the operations of selecting the topic or substance to be learned and setting the performance standards, with the collateral practical matter of setting some limit on how much can be devoted to instruction on the topic.

One may observe that these two sets of operations meet a formal or logical condition of teaching in that they make it possible to define the required gap between initial performance and the performance standard. Yet it does not follow that a teacher is logically required to perform the first set of operations. One may simply assume that a gap does exist and move on. Quite clearly, Stolurow hypothesizes that the first set of operations will increase the probability that learning will issue from teaching by decreasing the risk of choosing an inappropriate instrumental teaching act.

This hypothesis of Stolurow's is probably true, but to the writer's knowledge it has not been demonstrated to be true. When sufficient research has been conducted to determine that it is true, one criterion against which teaching performance can be appraised may have been partially defined. It will not have been completely defined because the style in which these operations are performed may be quite important to subsequent learning. For example, a recent study by Farr and Roelke (1969) indicates low correlations between clinical appraisals of reading subskills and standardized test appraisals. A teacher's choice between these two styles (or specific pattern of acts) of specifying entry behaviors might indeed have a bearing on learning outcomes.

Of the operations in the second set defined by Stolurow, selecting the topic

[1] The table on page 26 gives a summary of the major operations and their interaction, and may be of heuristic aid in reading the material which follows in this section.

is logically necessary to teaching, but only under purely didactic instruction is it an operation to be performed by the teacher. Pupils, after all, could perform this operation. But this is a stylistic matter. The specification of performance standards and the setting of time limits may be regarded as empirical matters—i.e., Stolurow must be hypothesizing that these operations increase efficiency, the probability of learning, or both. They deserve further research attention as possible criteria in the appraisal of teacher performance.

The second subgroup of operations in the pretutorial group, search and evaluation operations, bears directly on the selection of the instrumental teaching acts. In the *Socrates* model Stolurow details a number of subsets of operations, each associated with the number of instructional programs available for implementation via computer. For present purposes I would like to sidestep these subordinate operations and focus instead on the cognitive character of the major operations in this group.

The operations in sets 1 and 2—isolating student entry behaviors and setting the topic and performance standards—place many logical restrictions on the number of instrumental acts by the teacher which could be considered relevant. To put the matter in the language of Colladarci (1959), the range of relevant hypotheses is restricted. The thinking teacher would evaluate and select the instrumentality with the greatest probability of success. He would be McDonald's (1965) decision-making teacher. Psychologically, however, one would expect only very deliberate and very intellectual teachers to act so rationally. Perhaps a more realistic view is that of the behavior modification group, who would assume, I think, that the most heavily reinforced instrumentality would be selected from the hierarchy available.

Various theoretical viewpoints, as well as many criteria relevant to the performance of teaching, and hence to teacher education, are intrinsic to the search and evaluation operations. First, the range of instrumentalities, the scope of the response repertoire, available to the teacher seems distinctly criterial. For example, the difference between dull, routine teachers and stimulating, imaginative teachers may be at least partially defined on the basis of the scope of their response repertoires (Ryans, 1960). Second, if one holds an essentially rationalistic theoretical viewpoint about teaching—i.e., if one regards the teacher as an hypothesis-maker and a decision-maker—the *grounds* on which a teacher makes the selection may be regarded as criterial. In order for the teacher's performance to be criterial in this respect, the grounds selected must be those which take maximum advantage of what is known about pupil learning on a particular topic at whatever age level is involved. To put the matter another way, one must evaluate his instrumentalities against criteria drawn from his knowledge bases in child development, in educational psychology, and in the topical field. Third, if one holds a more Skinnerian viewpoint, the grounds on which the teacher makes the selection must be regarded as pragmatic. The question is which instrumentality has the maximum payoff in pupil performance. These grounds are obviously used in programmed learning.

Although rather different theoretical viewpoints may be brought to bear on the search and evaluation operations in teaching, these viewpoints are not necessarily in conflict with each other. The instrumentalities involved in teaching are of different magnitudes. Some are long and overarching teaching strategies (Smith *et al.*, 1964). Others involve moment to moment classroom moves. One can perhaps be fully ratiocinative about his teaching strategies and quite pragmatic about his moment to moment moves. For example, one may select the use of an advanced organizer in his strategy (Ausubel, 1962), and still make moment to moment moves contingent on pupil feedback. In any event, the establishment of firm criteria against which to appraise the search and evaluation operations in teaching is a fertile field for extended theory development and much empirical research.

A fair portion of the empirical research on pretutorial operations among teachers during the past ten years has been conducted at the Institute for Educational Research at Indiana University. All of this work has been conducted with simulated teaching tasks of a paper and pencil type, although audio tapes have been used to provide appropriate stimulus materials. The subject matter has been drawn largely from reading and arithmetic. Two types of tasks have been used. In one type, the teacher compares a sample of pupil performance to her own performance standards, then either makes a move relevant to defining the gap between the two or makes a move to select a relevant instrumentality. In the second type, the teacher organizes an instrumentality. The particular studies using these tasks have elsewhere been reported (Turner 1965 and 1968; Turner and Fattu, 1961; Turner, White, Quinn, and Smith, 1964), and I want here to focus on the broader outcomes.

First, teacher performance on such tasks shows a moderate positive correlation with general intelligence, block design performance, and teacher achievement in arithmetic and/or reading. A common factor associated with general information processing skills is probably involved. Performance is not associated with personal-social factors such as those in Ryans' Teacher Characteristic Schedule, or the Minnesota Teacher Attitudes Inventory (MTAI). Second, performance increases with relevant methods courses and student teaching, and also increases during the first two years of teaching experience, contingent primarily on the amount of supervision received during this period. Third, performance is positively associated with supervisory appraisals of teacher success and also with residual pupil achievement in arithmetic and reading. And fourth, performance levels are differentially distributed across school districts in such a way that those systems with the greater wealth and socioeconomic status (which also, incidentally, have the more elaborate systems of supervision) show much the higher performance levels.

The above evidence was originally interpreted to mean that the tasks constructed were construct-valid—i.e., that they measured skill in teaching. A different way to interpret the evidence might be to say that if one can develop instruments to assess the skills of the teacher in performing pretutorial operations, he may show that they hold a general relevance to the broader performances and outcomes of teaching. Increased research attention to these skills would surely yield substantial payoffs in defining criteria against which teaching performance can be appraised.

The "output" from the pretutorial operations in the *Socrates* model is the selection of a set of *tutorial* operations or a particular instrumentality. In the context of computer assisted instruction or programmed instruction, this instrumentality is, of course, a program. In broader perspective, the tutorial operations may be viewed as lying at a transition point between operations which comprise the structure of teaching and those which are stylistic. One *must* select an instrumentality in order to teach—i.e., this operation is logically necessary—but whether there are necessary structural elements within any instrumentality utilized in teaching is a good, but difficult, question. It may be examined with respect to the tutorial operations in the *Socrates* model.

There are six components in this model. One of these is the *task,* which is defined relative to two other components, *performance standards* and *stimulus* presentation or the cueing operation. The performance standards govern or moderate the teacher's cueing behavior. These cues are received by the *student* (or organism) who emits a *response,* for which *feedback* is then received. As Stolurow (1965) notes, the model is based on Woodworth's stimulus-organism-response paradigm with the addition of a feedback component. The question is whether any of the operations in the model are *necessary* to teaching.

There are two clearly overt and one primarily covert teacher operations in the model. Cueing or presenting a stimulus or stimulus array to the student is an overt operation. Giving feedback is also overt. The use of performance standards may be either overt or covert. Typically, the standards are covert and are revealed only when the teacher gives feedback. If one says "right" or "good" after a pupil response, he reveals that the response is congruent with his performance standard. Under these conditions performance standards are inferred entities. In some instances, however, they are observable. When a teacher demonstrates how a thing is to be done—for example, by threading a loom—he reveals performance standards; when he casts what is to be accomplished in "behavioral terms" he also explicates his standards. Whether he explicates them fully in either of the foregoing instances is a question which I shall avoid.

Of the above operations, feedback may be regarded as one of great empirical interest but as logically unnecessary to teaching. It may be a condition of student performance and of the maintenance of student responsiveness, but one can teach without it, although such teaching may be of little value on the criterion of eventuation in learning. The cueing operation, on the other hand, is logically necessary. The reason that it is issues from the premise that all teaching is dyadic. The dyad will not occur unless the teacher himself emits or in some other way provides for a response which serves as a stimulus to the pupil. That is how "interdependent" behavior gets going in teaching.

The residual question is whether performance standards are necessary to the tutorial operations in teaching. I think that the answer to this question is that performance criteria or standards are not necessary to teaching, but that they are necessary to the confirmation of learning under conditions of teaching. Hence performance criteria are necessary for knowing whether one's teaching acts are of any value. They are, therefore, of critical importance in teaching, although they are not logically necessary to it in a formal sense. To put the matter in a slightly different way, if one values only the teaching act, but has no regard for whether it eventuates in learning, then performance standards are irrelevant.

The central advantage of an examination of the structural aspects or operations in the tutorial processes provided by the *Socrates* model is that they provide a set of concepts, or conceptual hangers, at least, by which to cope with studies of teaching style. The latter studies emerge from a very wide variety of theoretical viewpoints, and if commonalities are to be seen among them a common structural framework is needed.

Style

If teaching were conducted only in the context of programmed instruction or computer assisted instruction, there would be only one type of teaching style. This style would be *task-relevant style* and would involve only variations in the operations conducted relative to the components or tasks which fall within the structure of teaching. Studies of variations in pretutorial operations, whether in cueing or in feedback, would fall within this stylistic domain; studies conducted within programmed instruction are an example. The current social organization of instruction introduces, however, a very different type of context, that of the teacher and the classroom group, of the legitimated leader and the "task-oriented" group. The way in which the leader operates with the group is his *leadership style.*

Without doubt, one of the great problems with research on teaching is that there is no logically necessary connection between the operations a leader performs with a group and the operations he performs as a teacher. A "task-oriented" group can work on any kind of task; the fact that in teaching the group task is learning about a particular topic is simply incidental from the viewpoint of an over-all consideration of leadership style. Teaching is merely another instance of leadership in task-oriented groups.

The history of research in teacher behavior and effectiveness is in considerable part a history of failing to make the distinction between leadership style and task-relevant style. Perhaps the reason for this failure is that there was neither much press toward making such a distinction nor much theoretical or empirical work to suggest that it should be made. The impetus provided by programmed instruction, by the dictum to define objectives in behavioral terms, and by efforts to attain a theory of instruction have made clear, however, that the task-relevant aspects of teaching style could be studied quite independently of other stylistic considerations. Collaterally, the recent work of Fiedler (1964, 1967, 1969) has made apparent that leadership style in teaching can be considered wholly apart from the teacher's task-relevant style—that is, simply as leadership in a task-oriented group.

In spite of the fact that there has been a modest amount of conscious distinction between these two types of style in the study of teacher behavior, as one looks across some of the major studies in the field since 1955, one is struck by the fact that some researchers have held to a substantial degree to the task-relevant side, others have been almost wholly on the leadership style side, while still others have held elements of both. In examining a selected few of these studies, a convenient way to order them is from those that focus primarily on task-relevant style toward those that focus on leadership style. The purpose of examining these studies is of course to locate potential criteria by which the performance of teaching may be appraised.

TASK-RELEVANT STYLE A severe limitation of many contemporary studies of teaching lies in the methodology adopted—the observation and categorization of classroom discourse and pupil-teacher interaction. Consequently, stylistic variations in pretutorial operations tend to be omitted from consideration, although there is every reason to think that the critical decisions in teaching are made during this phase of the process. For example, whether the teacher chooses an heuristic, inquiry, hypothesis-making approach or a more traditional didactic approach is presumably traceable into the pretutorial set of operations, since it is during this phase of instruction that the choice of instrumentality is made. Clearly, the work on heuristic teaching and teacher decision-making discussed by McDonald in Chapter 4 of this book is a start in this direction.

The tutorial operations in teaching are those observable in the classroom. They may be placed into three groups associated with the tutorial structures in the *Socrates* model: cueing, cue-response-feedback sequences, or "dyadic chaining" and feedback considered alone. In the classroom, performance standards must typically be inferred from the interrelations among the cue, the response, and the feedback.

CUEING Although there are now innumerable categorizing systems which involve simple teacher cueing behaviors in one way or another, I want to mention only three well-known ones: those by B. O. Smith (1961, 1966), Bellack and Davitz (1963), and Soar (1966b). These three capture what appear to be three of the principal attributes of cues—namely, (1) the logical operations entailed by the cue, (2) substance, and (3) affectivity. Other attributes of cues—such as criticality of the information they provide with respect to subsequent responding, redundancy, and linguistic structure—are open to study, of course, but the study of these matters has been restricted largely but not wholly to programmed instruction and the study of written materials.

CUEING: LOGICAL OPERATIONS An aspect of eliciting, soliciting, or cueing pupil responses which has been researched in teaching, but not sufficiently so, is the logical operation entailed by the cue. Identification of these operations appeared first in Smith's *The Logic of Teaching* (1961b), then in Bellack and Davitz's *The Language of the Classroom* (1963, 1965), and subsequently in the Ashner-Gallagher category system (1965) and in the Taba, Levine, and Elzey study (1966). The particular definitions attached to the operations vary among these studies, but that is not of consequence here. A key element in the Smith study, and in all of the subsequent studies, is that the solicitation, cue, or question from the teacher may be classified with respect to the kind of logical operation it requires of the pupil. Examples of such operations are: defining, describing, designating, stating, reporting, substituting, evaluating, opinioning, classifying, inferring, and explaining. These operations, as dimensions of the cue, hold two pertinent relationships in the *Socrates* model. First, they place determinants on the properties of the student response. One may, therefore, properly speak of the *congruence* between the operation called for in the cue and the operation performed in the response. Congruence is one of the variables studied by Bellack and Davitz, although not studied by Smith. Second, the reaction of the teacher to the congruence between the pupil's response and the cue implies the performance standards of the teacher.

A distinctly bizarre outcome of the Bellack and Davitz study was that the type of rating[2] reaction given by the teacher, classified as either positive or negative, remained constant at about 80 percent positive irrespective of the congruity or incongruity of the response of the pupil. Thus, if the cue called for a definition and the pupil opined rather than defined, there appeared to be a $4/5$ probability that he would be positively reinforced if the teacher made a rating response at all. This result suggests that the teachers in the Bellack and Davitz study, at least, did not respond to the logical dimensions of their own cueing behavior (Bellack and Davitz, 1965, p. 138). A question may clearly be raised about whether the performance standards of the teachers embraced any criteria bearing on logical operations.

Whether one regards the ability of a teacher to recognize and appropriately respond to the logical operations required by the cue as a criterial aspect of

[2] "Rating" means that the teacher had an evaluative component in his reaction—i.e., he "rated" the "goodness" of the response.

task-relevant style clearly depends on one's values. If one values even low-level critical thinking skills as a goal of instruction, however, one cannot escape considering appropriate teacher response to the logical operations performed by the pupil as a criterial aspect of teacher performance.

CUEING: SUBSTANCE The substantive aspects of cueing operations deal with specific facts, concepts, or principles in the subject matter taught. Moreover, substance is correlated with logical operations; for example, one defines concepts, reports facts, states or explains principles, and so on. Logical operations are general, however, while substantive operations are specific or topical and are difficult to cope with in studies of task-relevant style. Bellack and Davitz did, however, observe teacher reactions to the congruous and incongruous substantive responses of pupils. The positive reactions to both were again at about a probability of 80 percent.

Positive reactions at such a high probability level for incongruous responses raise a question about whether teachers "know the subject." That teachers should "know the subject" is, of course, a very old performance criterion for teachers. But the issue is not precisely whether they "know the subject." It is, rather, how they evidence their knowledge in a particular context. For example, it is well known that neither test knowledge of the subject one teaches nor one's college grade point average, presumably an index of knowledge, is very closely correlated with teacher effectiveness (Ryans, 1960). Perhaps the relevant evidence for whether a teacher "knows the subject'" does not lie in whether he can correctly answer the items on a test so much as it lies in his reactions to pupil responses to the cues he himself has emitted—in short, in the kind of performance standards he employs with respect to substantive responses from pupils. For example, the diagnostic skills of the teacher are evidenced in large part in the extent to which he isolates the discrepancies between the responses made by the students and his own performance standards. These discrepancies are then grouped and an appraisal is made of their relevance to learning the particular topic being considered. Both the isolation of discrepancies or errors and the appraisal of their relevance depend on the performance standards of the teacher. Moreover, one of the very interesting points which Stolurow (1965) raises with respect to performance standards in the tutorial model is that pupils learn or "internalize" them, and use them in turn to govern their own subsequent performance. If Stolurow's contention is an accurate one, and if diagnostic activity in teaching is important, a teacher's knowledge of the topical substance he teaches, as indicated through his apparent performance standards, is surely to be regarded as a criterial aspect of teacher performance.

CUEING: AFFECT In studies of classroom behavior, the affective properties of cueing are difficult to separate from the affective properties of feedback. Perhaps no separation should be attempted. There are two factors in a recent study by Soar (1966a), however, which are suggestive about the affectivity of cues. The first factor is "Teacher Criticism," which consists of three variables observed in the classrooms of some fifty-five elementary teachers:

Variable	*Factor Loading*
Teacher verbal hostility	—.76
Steady state teacher criticism	—.83
Pupil initiation following teacher criticism	—.74

The first variable was observed with the aid of the Fowler Hostility-Affection Schedule; the second was steady state 7–7 from Flanders' Classroom Interaction Analysis (CIA), and the third tallies in the 7–9 cell from Flanders' CIA. The composition of this factor clearly shows that teacher hostility and criticism, especially extended criticism, is associated with pupil responding—i.e., a cueing function is suggested. The nature of the pupil responding cannot be directly inferred from this factor.

The second factor is called "Pupil Hostility vs. Teacher Support and Pupil Interest," and consists of four variables:

Variable	*Factor Loading*
Pupil nonverbal hostility	.79
Pupil verbal hostility	.66
Teacher nonverbal affection	—.56
Pupil interest and attention rating	—.65

The first three variables were taken from the Fowler Schedule, the last variable from an adaptation of the Observation Schedule and Record Technique (OScAR). The composition of this factor suggests that teacher nonverbal affection is a positive correlate of pupil interest and an inverse correlate of pupil hostility. The maximum interpretation of the factor would be that teacher affection does not cue off hostility, but presumably minimizes hostility, while perhaps making it possible for pupils to pay attention.

Interestingly, both of the above factors were shown by Soar to be negatively related to pupil growth in arithmetic concepts and problems, while the second factor was, in addition, negatively associated with vocabulary growth and growth in creativity.

Although no one would regard the correlational evidence cited above as conclusive, it does indicate that the observation of the affectivity of the cues given by teachers can be profitably pursued. Moreover, it suggests that a specific dimension of the affectivity of cues, the affectional-hostility dimension, may be regarded as having very substantial potential as a criterion in the assessment of teacher performance.

CUEING: DYADIC CHAINS (SEQUENCING) Two more potential criteria in the assessment of teacher performance are associated with the dyadic chains which occur in classroom interaction. Such a chain involves a cycle of cues produced by the teacher and responses produced by the pupil. The first criterion was developed by Smith, Nuthall, *et al.*, in *Strategies of Teaching* (1966), and subsequently pursued by Nuthall (1968). Smith and company propose a unit of interaction, the *venture,* which incorporates (1) a subject matter objective, with a particular kind of cognitive operation implied, and (2) a maneuver on the part of the teacher to attain the objective with one or more pupils with whom he interacts. Nuthall has generated a method of diagramming "complex incidents" in the classroom which clearly shows the type of structure which underlies the venture. An example is shown in the accompanying figure.

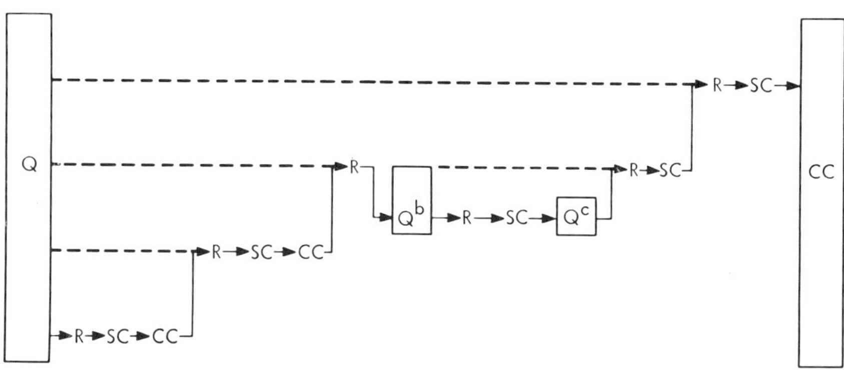

Diagram of a "complex incident," adapted from Nuthall (1965, p. 23). Q = initial question; Q^b and Q^c = subsidiary question; R = pupil response; SC = simple comment; CC = complex comment.

As suggested by the diagram, the maneuvering gets under way through an interrogative cue from the teacher, then proceeds through a chain of pupil responses, with simple and complex comments or cues from the teacher, toward a termination point, represented in this particular diagram by a complex comment from the teacher. Under Smith's concept of venture, this complex comment would signal that the particular substantive objective had been reached. Ventures have been typed by Smith *et al.* according to the cognitive operation implicit to the substantive outcome—for example, conceptual venture, causal venture, procedural venture, rule venture, and so on. A conceptual venture, for instance, might involve exploration and analysis of a concept in anthropology. The maneuver adopted by the teacher in a venture might involve several types of *moves.* For example, in a conceptual venture, the moves might involve giving instances (instantial moves), describing (descriptive moves), comparing the concept with others (comparative moves), and so on.

At the present level of development, neither the types of ventures nor the types of moves performed by teachers in a particular type of venture can be shown to be unequivocally associated with student learning. For example, a recent experiment by Nuthall (1968) indicated that although a particular maneuver or strategy of teaching may facilitate the learning of one particular concept, it may not facilitate the learning of another. Thus, the consequences of particular maneuvers are at present hard to predict since they interact with the substantive topic. Nonetheless, the way in which the teacher maneuvers within a particular topical venture may be regarded as potentially criterial for the assessment of teacher performance, although substantial work remains to be done to specify relationships between particular kinds of maneuvers in particular types of ventures in specific subject areas.

A second set of criteria of potential use in the assessment of teacher performance may be derived from a recent study by Denny (1966) on classroom creativity factors among thirty sixth grade teachers. Of the three sets of variables developed by Denny, two sets, general structuring and specific structuring for creativity, may be generally identified with dyadic chaining, although very specific moves in such chains cannot be identified under the observational system used. General structuring includes (1) initiation—the extent to which the teacher permits pupils to initiate activity; (2) approach—the way in which the teacher paces and moves instruction along (the dyadic chain); (3) adaptation—the extent to which the teacher differentiates for individual pupils; and (4) variation—the total variation in the stimulus arrays used. Specific structuring includes (1) divergency—the extent to which the teacher gives cues which encourage or stimulate divergent pupil responding; (2) uniqueness—the extent to which the teacher uses materials in a unique way, and (3) unusual responses—the extent to which the teacher encourages or reinforces unusual (creative) responses.

Among the specific variables noted above, three—initiation, adaptation, and divergency—show the most consistent and statistically significant relationships ($p < .01$) to residual pupil gain on various tests adapted from Guilford's battery of creativity tests. These three variables provide a different perspective on the way in which the teacher moves than do the studies by Smith and Nuthall. Initiation deals, in essence, with the extent to which pupils may participate in the various moves made, while adaptation deals with the way in which interaction is spread across members of the class. Neither of these variables deals with the particular sequence of instruction, but rather, with who is participating in the sequence. The third variable, divergency, may be recognized as primarily an attribute of the cues provided by the teacher. Of interest is the fact that the reinforcement of unusual (creative) responses was not closely associated with residual gain on the creativity tests.

Like the work of Smith and Nuthall, Denny's work may not be regarded as conclusive in providing relevant criteria against which to appraise the performance of teachers. Nonetheless, Denny has developed highly specific variables which apparently relate to changes in pupil creativity in the classroom, and has therefore demonstrated the potential utility of these variables as criteria against which teacher performance may be appraised.

FEEDBACK As a concept, feedback presents little difficulty in the study of teaching style. It may be composed either of affective information returned to the student following a response, or of information of an essentially cognitive type which tells the student about the "correctness" of his response, or both. The operations by which "feedback" may be defined in observing teacher classroom behavior, however, permit less clarity. A part of the difficulty lies in determining the point at which feedback leaves off and cueing behavior begins. Moreover, in some types of observation systems, such as Flanders' Classroom Interaction Analysis, feedback and cueing behaviors both slide off toward a variable which also defines leadership style, namely, the indirect-direct (*i*/*d*) ratio.

There is in classroom instruction, moreover, another difficulty with feedback. In classroom discussion most teachers make a general solicitation of the class but permit only one individual to respond. Technically, the teacher returns feedback only to this individual, while the nonresponding portion of the class gets, at best, vicarious feedback or vicarious reinforcement.

Some of the early studies of feedback in the classroom, such as that by Mech, Hurst, Auble, and Fattu (1953), showed significant relationships, under experimental conditions, between teacher feedback and pupil learning in arithmetic. Subsequent behavior modification studies, such as that by Orme and Purnell (1968), very strongly suggest that systematic positive reinforcement of selected pupil behaviors, administered largely on an individual basis, brings about very great modifications in pupil behavior. On the other hand, in Bellack's and Davitz's study noted earlier, teacher reactions, classified as positive or negative, were unrelated to pupil learning; in the Denny study, teacher reinforcement of unusual responses was unrelated to creativity change, as noted earlier.

On the surface, the Flanders' *i*/*d* ratio looks like a ratio of positive to negative (or perhaps punitive) feedback, and at least at present, the evidence appears to be that somewhat greater levels of positive in proportion to negative reinforcement have salubrious effects on learning (Campbell and Barnes, 1969). At the root, however, the *i*/*d* ratio is an ambiguous entity. Categories 6 (teacher directions) and 7 (criticism) in the Flanders system represent cueing as well as some feedback. Categories 1 (accepts feeling) and 2 (praises or encourages) are probably affective feedback categories, while category 3 (expands pupil response) is feedback of a cognitive type. As Soar (1966a) has shown, however, the indirect categories (1, 2, 3) load on a factor orthogonal to the direct categories (6, 7), and it is the factor containing the direct categories which is inversely related to achievement, while the factor containing the indirect categories is not related to achievement. Thus, the *i*/*d* ratio confounds the question of which particular variables are linked to achievement and perhaps cannot be used as evidence that positive feedback is associated with pupil learning.

Perhaps the key to understanding the rather murky relationships which surround the role of teacher feedback in the classroom group lies in considering the precise relationships between pupil responses and teacher feedback. In experimental or intervention studies such as those by Mech, Hurst, Auble, and Fattu (1953) and by Orme and Purnell (1968), relatively close control is exercised over the particular type of response that is to be reinforced. In observational or "naturalistic" studies, however, it is typically not known which particular classes of pupil response the teacher is reinforcing. The data from the Bellack and Davitz study is a case in point. There is no question but that positively reinforcing both congruent and incongruent pupil response at 80 percent probability is irrational teacher behavior if one assumes that the pupil response classes to which the teacher is responding involve either substance or the logical operation on the substance. The teacher behavior in question is not irrational, however, if one assumes that what the teacher is reinforcing is simply pupil response as a gross entity. To have discussion one must have pupils who respond. If an experimentor places recording equipment in a classroom to record the discussion, the obvious task for the teacher is to maintain discussion. A rational strategy for maintaining discussion is to reinforce pupils who discuss, irrespective of the specific content of their remarks.

From a theoretical viewpoint, there is perhaps little question that teacher feedback operations are a criterial aspect of teaching performance. Practically speaking, however, there appear to be grounds for questioning whether an adequate set of procedures has been developed for defining precisely what it is about teacher feedback operations that is to be regarded as criterial. Hence, one may regard stylistic variations in the way in which feedback is handled by the teacher as potentially criterial, but too full of puzzles at present to occupy full criterial status.

Leadership Style

Although there is no logically necessary connection between leadership style and task-relevant style in teaching, that there are important empirical relationships between the two can hardly be questioned. Broadly speaking, leadership style embraces the way in which the leader orients toward the group *vis-à-vis* the task or tasks to be accomplished by the group. This orientation may be described in a very wide number of ways—for example, as task-oriented versus person-oriented, as democratic versus authoritarian, as child-centered versus subject-centered (or teacher-centered), as permissive

Criterial Domains and Operations	*Status of Operation or Stylistic Variable if Convergent, Divergent, or Affective Outcome Is Sought*	*Operations X Style* — *Task-Relevant Style*								*Leadership Style*
Domain: Structure										
Pretutorial Operations										
Inputs										
Select topic *	Analytic									X
Identify entry performance †	Hypothesized									X
gap	Analytic									
Set terminal performance level (standard) *	Hypothesized									
Set time limit *	Practical consideration									X
Identify relevant personality and aptitude variates †	Hypothesized									
Search and Evaluation										
Select teaching instrumentality	Analytic					X	X			X
Tutorial Operations										
task: Cueing (stimuli presentation)	Analytic	X	X	X	X	X	X	X	X	X
task: (Permitting student response)	Hypothesized									
task: Application of performance standard	Hypothesized	X	X	X	X	X	X	X	X	X
task: Feedback	Hypothesized							X	X	
Domain: Task-relevant Style										
Inter-teacher variability in:										
Logical operation required by cue	Hypothesized	(1)								
Substantive accuracy of cue	Hypothesized		(2)							
Affectivity of cue	Hypothesized			(3)						
Cue sequencing	Hypothesized				(4)					
Cue initiation (pupil vs. teacher)	Hypothesized					(5)				
Cue uniqueness	Hypothesized						(6)			
Congruity of feedback with cue demands	Hypothesized							(7)		
Affectivity of feedback	Hypothesized								(8)	
Domain: Leadership Style										
Personal-socially oriented, permissive vs. task-oriented, traditional	Contingent upon 1. leader-member relations 2. position power 3. task structure									(leadership)

* Set 2
† Set 1

versus traditional, as direct versus indirect, and so on. By whatever terms they are described, the referents involve a wide range of teacher characteristics and associated classroom behaviors, such as the extent to which the teacher permits pupils to formulate the tasks to be accomplished, the broad types of instrumentalities which the teacher sees as permissible in the classroom, the flexibility (looseness, tightness) of the teacher's performance standards, the amount of affective supportive behavior given, the broad cueing style adopted (e.g., inquiry-oriented versus answer-oriented) (Snow, 1969), and the management of feedback relative to its consequences for group relationships as well as for task learning.

Studies involving the leadership styles of teachers are very numerous, very confusing in the array of variables and procedures used, and generally inconclusive. These studies have been extensively dealt with in the recent past by such able persons as Withall and Lewis (1963), Getzels and Jackson (1963), Ryans (1963), and Flanders (1969), and I will not attempt to review the studies here. Rather, what I want to do is briefly examine Fiedler's contingency theory of leadership effectiveness because it seems to offer some hope of bringing theoretical order out of the disarray which seems to me to characterize the leadership style studies in education.

The Fiedler model (1964, 1967, 1969) involves only four variables, one characterizing the leader, and three the situation: (1) *leadership style*—characterized along a task-oriented vs. person-oriented dimension (the more task-oriented person may be viewed as somewhat more authoritarian, more direct in approach, perhaps more "businesslike," whereas the person-oriented person is more permissive, more supportive, more indirect in his approach); (2) the *"position-power"* of the leader—the degree to which the organizational position he occupies accords authority over members of the group and sanctions which may be applied with respect to their behavior; (3) *leader-member relationships*—the extent to which the leader and members are in accord, get along, or like each other; and (4) *task structure*—the degree to which the task has definite, immediately verifiable outcomes as opposed to outcomes the precise "goodness" of which cannot be immediately confirmed. An example of a task with high task structure would be spelling; an example of low task structure would be speculating on the consequences of the immediate withdrawal of the United States from the Vietnam conflict.

Under the contingency model of leadership effectiveness, the extent to which a task-oriented as opposed to a person-oriented leadership style will be effective depends on the arrangement of the three situational variables. Among these three variables, leader-member relationships is identified by Fiedler as exerting the greatest influence, with task structure second, and position-power exerting least influence. If each of the latter variables is dichotomized, an eight-cell arrangement is produced, which, if hierarchically arranged, yields the following diagram.

Leader-member relations	good				poor			
Task structure	structured		unstructured		structured		unstructured	
Position-power	strong	weak	strong	weak	strong	weak	strong	weak
	1	2	3	4	5	6	7	8

By plotting many correlations between leadership style and the effectiveness of group performance in each of the cells, Fiedler has produced some most interesting results. When the situation is favorable to the leader—i.e., when leader-member relationships are good—when task structure is high, and when position-power is strong, as in cell 1, then the more task-oriented leader is the more effective leader. This remains true through cell 3. However, as task structure decreases and position-power weakens, as in cell 4, effective group performance begins to strongly correlate with the person-oriented leader. This remains true through cell 6. Thereafter the correlations shift, and in cells 7 and 8 the task-oriented leader again becomes the more effective. In general, when the situation is very favorable to the leader or when it is very unfavorable to the leader, a task-oriented style is more effective, but when the situation is of mixed favorability, the person-oriented leader is the more effective.

The value of a contingency model of leadership effectiveness with respect to the criteria against which teaching performance may be appraised is, at this point, wholly heuristic. The model clearly suggests that past studies of leadership style in teaching which have not taken into account the primary situational variables upon which the effectiveness of leadership style is apparently contingent are at the maximum uninterpretable and at the minimum of slight external validity. Collaterally, if leadership style is to become a criterial aspect of teacher performance, careful separation of such matters as variation in teacher position-power across grade levels and in different types of communities, variation in task structure within and between substantive areas, and variation in relationships between the teacher and his students will have to be taken into account. The criterion is not whether the teacher exhibits or fails to exhibit a particular kind of leadership style—i.e., "permissive," "democratic," or "indirect"—but rather whether the style he exhibits is congruent with the leadership style established to be effective for the conditions under which he teaches.

THE PROBLEM OF TREATMENT VALIDITY

A preservice teacher education program is always composed of a selected set of experiences or treatments which lie along a time line or time continuum.

The point of origin of the time continuum may be as early as the freshman year of college, depending on the program, while the end point falls at the end of the fourth or fifth year of college-university work and is followed by the in-service program time continuum which runs parallel with a continuum of formal teaching experience in a school.

The problem of treatment validity is the problem of demonstrating significant relationships between the treatments which fall on the preservice continuum and the criteria for teaching performance which most relevantly apply during the first through the third year of formal teaching experience. This particular way of stating the problem presumes that teacher education implicitly involves a kind of transfer of training paradigm in which the learning trials are run during a preservice period and the test trials during the early years of formal teaching experience. The prediction is always that positive transfer will occur. Structurally, the transfer of training paradigm is undoubtedly an accurate one for teacher education. In practice, however, teacher education offers much greater methodological and theoretical complexity than the standard transfer experiment. To cope with these complexities, the teacher educator and the researcher in teacher education need to adopt strategies. The point of these strategies is, on the one hand, to validate preservice educational treatments and, on the other, to optimize the performance of a particular group of teachers against a set of performance criteria. As suggested in the introductory section, to "optimize" the performance of a particular group of teachers means, from a psychological viewpoint, to show a comparative performance advantage, while from an economic and social viewpoint, it means that the teachers produce a maximum of socially valuable behaviors in students.

There are two basic strategies for simultaneously validating preservice education treatments and optimizing teacher performance during the earlier years of teaching experience. Both strategies are primarily psychological in character, although each intertwines methodological and theoretical considerations. The first of these strategies involves what I shall call "movables" and the conditions of practice, while the second involves Gagne-like assumptions about the hierarchical nature of specific criterial components in the performance of teaching.

Both the treatments on the preservice time continuum and aspects of formal teaching experience are "movables." For example, a reasonably common characteristic of "experimental" teacher education during the late 1950s and early 1960s was the tendency to push the treatments in the preservice program forward toward the junior, senior, or even the graduate year of teacher education. Frequently accompanying this move was a grouping or blocking of particular courses, especially methods courses. Strategically speaking, the forward movement of such courses decreases the time lag between the methods treatment, the practice in student teaching of the skills and knowledges acquired in the methods treatment, and the on-the-job performance of teachers. Such a decrease in the time lag in turn potentially decreases the number of intervening variables which can interfere with the memory of the skills and knowledges. The primary advantage of this type of move seems to me to be methodological—that is, it shrinks the time interval between the treatment and the application of the criterion, and thereby improves the probability of showing a significant association between the two if the treatment has any validity at all with respect to the criterion.

A second kind of movable are those various aspects of teaching experience which may be stretched backward, so to speak, to run parallel with the preservice program. The teaching experience may be intense, as in internships or in student teaching, or it may be less intense and more widely distributed over the treatments, as might be the case with microteaching and, in decreasing order, with stimulus- or problem-posing films or video tapes and simulated teaching tasks of a paper and pencil type. The backward movement of teaching experience in parallel with preservice treatments is of strategic advantage primarily in that it makes possible practice, with correction, of various skills under conditions which are in varying degrees similar to those which are likely to be encountered in later formal teaching experience. Since maximum transfer of training occurs when the learning or treatment trials are highly similar to the test trials, moving teaching experience, or aspects of it, into the preservice program holds the possibility of greatly enhancing the association between the treatments and the criterion.

The strategy involving movables and the conditions of practice described immediately above is a widely recognized one in teacher education, and it certainly holds promise for optimizing the relationships between the treatments in teacher education and the subsequent performance of teaching. The difficulty, however, is that such a strategy will have its optimizing effect on the relationship between any particular treatment and any particular criterion of teacher performance. Thus, if the performance criterion utilized by teacher educators happens to be one that is inversely related to pupil productivity, the valued social outcomes of teaching could be substantially damaged even though the psychological objective might have in some sense been met. The possibility of this type of outcome seems somewhat bizarre, yet it is perfectly conceivable that a group of teacher educators could work very diligently to produce in their students a highly person-oriented leadership style, which, under subsequent actual teaching conditions, was inversely associated with leadership effectiveness.

The second strategy for validating treatments in the preservice program and optimizing criterial performance in teaching begins with the assumption that the criteria against which teaching performance is to be appraised have been operationally defined and are in some degree valid, and subsequently incorporates the Gagne-like assumption of a learning hierarchy. For example, the performance criterion may be that the teacher should be able both to discriminate the congruence of the response of the student with respect to logical operations required by the cue and to supply feedback appropriate to the student's response. In order to perform this operation, one might hypothesize (1) that the teacher must be able to distinguish among classes of logical operations—e.g., to separate "defining" from "opining"; (2) that he must be able to identify instances belonging to one class as opposed to another; (3) that he must hold some criteria concerning the permissible variability of instances in a class—e.g., he must have some criterion for discerning the characteristics of various types of definitions; (4) that he must be able to frame a cue which makes clear which logical operation is being called for; (5) that he must listen to the response and retain its characteristics (Snow, 1969); (6) that he must be able to compare quickly the response characteristics to his performance standard; (7) that he must diagnose the significance of the discrepancy between the performance standard and the response characteristics, if any exists; and (8) that he must be able to gauge the impact of his feedback response on the student and on other students. Indeed, the latter ability is very complex and probably could itself be analyzed into component skills.

The point is, however, that once a valid performance criterion for teachers has been isolated, the validity of the treatments of a teacher education program can be increased by addressing the component parts of the criterion skill. As may be noted in the above example, the component skills may have a kind of prerequisite structure so that the performance of certain ones of them is predicated on the ability to perform others. In short, some type of learning hierarchy exists. The members of this hierarchy may be collaterally distributed down or programmed across various treatments, with the final integration of the skill occurring at a point late in the treatment sequence.

If one uses this particular method of programming component skills across courses, with a final integration late in the treatment sequence, student performance at the final level of the treatment may be employed as the predictor of on-the-job performance. If a significant association is found, and if, in fact, the subordinate treatments contribute component skills prerequisite to the integrated performance at the final treatment level, then each of the treatments subordinate to the final treatment may be interpreted as sharing in the validity of the final treatment. One may observe in this light that if student teaching is to be the final treatment in the sequence of treatments, it should serve as a place in which the final integration of teaching skills can occur and as a point at which the predictor variables which are to be related to on-the-job performance can be generated.

A third strategy for treatment validation may be regarded either as a form of the second strategy or perhaps as a hybrid of the first and second strategies, and may be called the "movable criterion" strategy. It is useful for working with the less observable aspects of teaching, but at the same time its utility is heavily dependent on the particular procedures by which the criteria for teacher performance are defined.

To be "movable" a performance criterion either must itself elicit or cue off components of the criterial performance or must be capable of isolating the criterial aspects of performance elicited by some set of stimuli external to itself. Examples of devices which are at least intended as movable criteria which elicit criterial aspects of performance are Ryans' teacher behavior correlate scales—Xco (warm, friendly), Yco (responsible, businesslike) and Zco (stimulating, imaginative) (Ryans, 1961)—and Turner's Teaching Tasks (Turner, 1968; Turner, White, Quinn, and Smith, 1964). The Ryans' scales may be regarded as measures of leadership style, and are probably associated with leadership style dimensions similar to those noted by Fiedler—at least the recent work of Kerlinger and Pedhazur (1967) so suggests. The Ryans' scales were developed by correlating paper and pencil items with observed teacher classroom behavior. To the extent that the items in the correlate scales sample components of the universe of behavior originally observed, and to the extent that the behaviors originally observed are regarded as criterial, the correlate scales may also be regarded as criterial. The Turner "tasks," on the other hand, were validated primarily by demonstrating their association with a variety of criteria relevant to teaching, as noted in the earlier discussion on the pretutorial aspects of teaching.

The difficulty with two examples of movable criteria noted above, and perhaps with all similar criteria, is that they rarely capture a sufficiently broad or exhaustive set of behaviors to be regarded as completely convincing criteria. To put the matter another way, they are relevant and suggestive criteria, but they lack adequate power.

Examples of movable criteria which depend on stimuli external to themselves in order to elicit the required behavior are the various observational devices such as Flanders' CAI, Denny's Classroom Creativity Observation Schedule, and, indeed, all the myriad of such instruments noted in *Mirrors of Behavior* (Simon and Boyer, 1967). The utility of such instruments in a teacher education program depends on whether some kind of teaching experience can be made available in the teacher education program. There is, moreover, a difficulty with these instruments. None of them at present yields normed or standardized data; the level of behavior of a particular kind—e.g., "indirect behavior"—to be regarded as criterial is left unspecified. Soar (1966a), for example, has noted that the relationship between teacher indirectness and pupil learning may be curvelinear (inverted U). If this were to be true, then assuming that greater degrees of indirectness stand for "better" leadership, style would be erroneous.

In spite of the shortcomings of the various types of movable criteria discussed above, we should regard them as distinct advances in devices by which to help validate the treatments in teacher education programs. Certainly they are superior to the criterial guesswork that has long characterized teacher education.

A type of movable criterion that runs in what seems to be a kind of reverse direction from those noted above was recently developed by Trojcak (1969) in a study of preservice teacher education in science. The aspect of criterial teacher performance involved may be regarded either as the organization of the teaching instrumentality, or, more liberally, as the organization of potential moves in a dyadic chain. In the study Trojcak gave a different degree of instruction about Gagne's learning continuum to each of five groups ($n = 11$ in each group) of preservice teachers. Each person in each group subsequently developed a programmed learning program on friction for use with fourth graders. Each program was then randomly assigned to a randomly selected (within a school) group of five fourth-grade pupils, with no previous instruction about friction, and pupil post-test performance over the program content was obtained. Differences in the performance levels of the pupils who had taken the programs prepared by the students in each of the five groups were then tested statistically. Incredibly enough, there was a general linear relationship between pupil performance and the degree of instruction given to the preservice teacher, with the statistical differences appearing between the most highly trained students and those least trained.

The important point about this study is not, however, that the pupil performance was linearly related to the level of training of the preservice teachers, but that the criteriality of the preservice teachers' performance was tested directly against pupil performance. Thus, in this case, pupil performance turned out to be the movable criterion. The possibility of moving pupil performance is perhaps not very great in most programs of teacher education, but when it can be moved, it provides a quite convincing criterion against which to judge the validity of the preservice treatment.

SUMMARY

For a preservice teacher education program to be demonstrably valid, relationships must be established between the treatments delivered in the program and performance criteria in teaching. For the performance criteria to be valid, they must be shown to be either logically necessary to teaching or associated with pupil learning attributable to teaching.

To develop relevant performance criteria, teaching may be viewed as composed of three domains—structure, style, and substance. The structure of teaching embraces the logically necessary operations in teaching and the empirical operations which may be hypothesized to be criterial if teaching is to eventuate in learning. Variations in the performance of the criterial operations in teaching are to be regarded as statements about the task-relevant style of the teacher. Particular variations in task-relevant style may be regarded as criterial when they can be shown to be associated with pupil learning. Task-relevant style in teaching is to be separated from the leadership style of the teacher, to which it holds no intrinsic connection. Like task-relevant style, however, leadership style can be regarded as criterial in teaching only when the latter can be shown to be associated with pupil learning under a particular set of classroom conditions.

To demonstrate relationships between performance criteria in teaching and treatments in preservice teacher education programs, the teacher educator must develop strategies which enhance the probability of showing these relationships. These strategies include moving the treatments temporarily closer to the criterion trials, moving fractional parts of the criterion trials backward toward the treatments, using movable correlates of the criteria down into the preservice program, and having preservice teachers develop operations which may be vicariously tested against pupil achievement.

REFERENCES

Aschner, M. J. McQ., and James J. Gallagher, 1965. *Aschner-Gallagher System for Classifying Thought Processes in the Context of Classroom Verbal Interaction.* Urbana: Institute for Research on Exceptional Children, University of Illinois.

Ausubel, David P., 1962. "A Subsumption Theory of Meaningful Verbal Learning." *Journal of General Psychology,* 66:312–24.

Bellack, Arno, *et al.,* 1963. *The Language of the Classroom,* Part One. New York: Institute for Psychological Research, Teachers' College, Columbia University.

———, 1965. *The Language of the Classroom,* Part Two. New York: Institute for Psychological Research, Teachers' College, Columbia University.

Campbell, J. R., and C. W. Barnes, 1969. "Interaction Analysis—A Breakthrough?" *Phi Delta Kappan,* June 1969, pp. 587–90.

Colladarci, Arthur P., 1959. "The Teacher as Hypothesis-Maker." *California Journal for Instructional Improvement,* 2:3–6.

Denny, David A., 1966. *A Preliminary Analysis of an Observation Schedule Designed to Identify the Teacher-Classroom Variables which Facilitate Pupil Creative Growth.* CRP No. 6–8325–2–12–1. Bloomington: U.S. Office of Education. Indiana University.

Farr, Roger, and Patricia Roelke, 1969. "Measuring Subskills in Reading." Bloomington: Indiana University (Mimeo).

Fiedler, Fred, 1964. "A Contingency Model of Leadership Effectiveness," in *Advances in Experimental Social Psychology,* Leonard Berkowitz, ed. New York: Academic Press.

———, 1967. *A Theory of Leadership Effectiveness.* New York: McGraw-Hill Book Company.

———, 1969. "Style or Circumstance: The Leadership Enigma." *Psychology Today,* 2:38–43.

Flanders, Ned, 1962. *Teacher Influence, Pupil Attitudes and Achievement.* Ann Arbor: University of Michigan.

———, 1969. "Teacher Effectiveness." *Encyclopedia of Educational Research,* 4th ed. New York: The Macmillan Company, pp. 1423–38.

Getzels, J. W., and P. W. Jackson, 1963. "The Teacher's Personality and Characteristics," in *Handbook of Research on Teaching,* N. L. Gage, ed. Chicago: Rand McNally and Co.

Kerlinger, Fred N., and Elazar J. Pedhazur, 1967. *Attitudes and Perceptions of Desirable Traits and Behavior of Teachers.* USOE CRP Final Report.

McDonald, Frederick J., 1965. *Educational Psychology.* Belmont, Cal.: Wadsworth Publishing Co., Chap. 2.

Mech, E. V., F. M. Hurst, J. D. Auble, and N. A. Fattu, 1953. *An Experimental Analysis of Patterns of Differential Verbal Reinforcement in Classroom Situation.* Bulletin of the School of Education, Indiana University, Vol. 29, No. 5, September 1953.

Nuthall, Graham, 1968. "An Experimental Comparison of Alternative Strategies for Teaching Concepts." *American Educational Research Journal,* 5:561–84, November 1968.

———, and P. J. Lawrence, 1965. *Thinking in the Classroom.* Wellington, New Zealand: New Zealand Council for Research.

Orme, Michael E. J., and Richard E. Purnell, 1968. "Behavior Modification and Transfer in an Out-of-Control Classroom." Paper delivered at 1968 AERA Convention, Chicago (Mimeo).

Ryans, David G., 1960. "Teacher Effectiveness." *Encyclopedia of Educational Research.* Chicago: Rand McNally, and Co.

———, 1961. *The Characteristics of Teachers.* Washington: American Council on Education.

———, 1963. "Teacher Behavior Theory and Research: Implications for Teacher Education." *Journal of Teacher Education,* 14:274–93, September 1963.

Simon, Anita, and E. G. Boyer, 1967. *Mirrors for Behavior,* Special ed. Philadelphia: Research for Better Schools and Center for the Study of Teaching.

Smith, B. O., 1961(a). "A Concept of Teaching," in *Language and Concepts in Education,* B. O. Smith and Robert H. Ennis, eds. Chicago: Rand, McNally and Co.

——— *et al.,* 1961(b). *The Logic of Teaching.* Urbana: Bureau of Educational Research, College of Education, University of Illinois.

——— *et al.,* 1966. *A Study of the Strategies of Teaching.* Urbana: Bureau of Educational Research, College of Education, University of Illinois.

Snow, Richard E., 1969. "Heuristic Teaching." *Program Plan and Budget Re-*

quest. Palo Alto, Cal.: Stanford Center for Research and Development in Teaching, Stanford University, October 1969, pp. 68–73.

Soar, Robert S., 1966(a). "Teacher-Pupil Interaction and Pupil Growth." Paper delivered at 1966 AERA Convention, Chicago.

———, 1966(b). *An Integrative Approach to Classroom Learning.* Philadelphia: Temple University.

Stolurow, Lawrence M., 1965. "Model the Master Teacher or Master the Teaching Model," in *Learning and the Educational Process,* J. D. Krumboltz, ed. Chicago: Rand McNally and Co.

Taba, Hilda, Samuel Levine, and Freeman F. Elzey, 1966. *Thinking in Elementary School Children.* Final Report CRP No. 1574, San Francisco State College.

Trojcak, Doris A., 1969. *Five Stages of Instruction for Sequencing Science Activities According to Gagne's Learning Model.* Unpublished Doctoral Dissertation, Indiana University, June 1969.

Turner, R. L., 1965. *The Acquisition of Teaching Skills in Elementary School Settings.* Bulletin of the School of Education, Indiana University.

———, 1968. *Differential Association of Elementary School Teacher Characteristics with School System Types.* Final Report USOE CRP 2579, September 1968.

———, and N. A. Fattu, 1960. *Skill in Teaching: A Reappraisal of the Concepts and Strategies in Teacher Effectiveness Research.* Bulletin of the School of Education, Indiana University, Vol. 36, No. 3, May 1960.

———, 1961. *Skill in Teaching Assessed on the Criterion of Problem Solving.* Bulletin of the School of Education, Indiana University.

Turner, R. L., K. P. White, E. Quinn, and N. Smith, 1964. *Skill in Teaching Assessed on the Criterion of Problem-Solving: Three Studies.* Bulletin of the School of Education, Indiana University.

Withall, John, and W. W. Lewis, 1963. "Social Interaction in the Classroom," in *Handbook of Research on Teaching,* N. L. Gage, ed. Chicago: Rand McNally and Co.

3

Research on Teacher Performance Criteria

BARAK ROSENSHINE/NORMA FURST

This review is an admission that we know very little about the relationship between classroom behavior and student gains. It is a plea for more research on teaching. It is also a plea to educational researchers and to teacher educators to devote more time and money to the study of classroom teaching.

In the first section of this paper we discuss the limitations of our knowledge about teaching, and acknowledge that sufficient information is not available on the relationship between a teacher's behavior and student learning in the classroom to design adequate programs in teacher education. In the second section we discuss the major results of one of the more promising areas of research on teaching—those studies which attempted to relate observed teacher classroom behaviors to measures of student achievement. In the third section we discuss some of the issues and problems in research on teaching and offer suggestions for future research. We regard the third section as the most important because a great deal of the research we propose can take place within the context of teacher education programs. In order for such research to be conducted, educational researchers will have to give of their time and of their skills. We hope that this chapter will persuade them to do so.

The authors are greatly indebted to Lilian Katz, Robert Stake, and Herbert Walberg, University of Illinois; Graham Nuthall, University of Canterbury, New Zealand; and Barbara Rosenshine for criticizing earlier drafts of this chapter. This review was partly supported by USOE Grant 9B–010 to Temple University.

PERFORMANCE CRITERIA IN TEACHER EDUCATION

The use of "performance criteria" in the training of teachers is a relatively recent development in teacher education. In most instances, the term "performance criteria" refers to specific teacher behaviors such as "asking evaluative questions" or "providing reinforcement of student answers." Usually teacher behavior is observed in a classroom or in a mini-classroom situation. Sometimes, however, the term "performance criteria" has a wider range of meaning than observable teacher behavior. It has been used to refer to criterion performance as indicated on an examination or by the completion of a project, or by participation in a discussion. The usual connotation of the term, however, is the specification of a teacher's behavior while he interacts with children in a classroom. The specification of behavior represents a radical shift from the traditional, vague objectives of "providing meaningful experiences," "educating the whole child," and "providing for individual differences." The new focus upon denotable actions is praiseworthy.

The term "performance criteria" and similar terms dominate the model teacher education programs funded by the U.S. Office of Education. For example, the program developed by the Northwest Regional Laboratory stresses "instructional experiences that lead to both development and personalization of competencies" (Schalock, 1968, p. 6). In the Michigan State Model, some 2700 modules are specified, many of which are evaluated in terms of trainee behaviors (Houston, 1968). The Massachusetts Model is explicit in requiring "the specification of instructional and program goals in terms of behaviors to be exhibited by the trainee" (Allen, 1968, p. 17). The Syracuse proposal claims that "the model program specifies its objectives in behavioral terms, provides situations where these behaviors can be learned, and when behaviors are manifest, assesses their quality and character in behavioral terms" (Hough, 1968, p. 23). The Teachers College Model developed 818 educational specifications (Joyce, 1968).

This focus on performance criteria probably developed from two sources. The first is the emphasis in the current literature on behavioral objectives in instruction. The second source is undoubtedly the series of experimental studies which have been conducted in teacher education. These studies were designed to determine whether training procedures could modify the behavior of the teacher as measured by systematic observation. The results of these investigations indicated that training procedures which focused on denotable, specific behaviors were more effective than traditional methods courses in changing teacher behavior. Hence an emphasis on specifics–i.e., on performance criteria–seemed desirable to the planners of the model programs.

Although hundreds of teacher performance criteria are specified in the U.S.

Office of Education's Model Teacher Education Programs, the programs do not describe how these particular criteria were chosen. None of the proposals contains a detailed review of the literature upon which the model builders based their decisions.

Descriptive Classroom Studies as a Source of Performance Criteria

Lacking adequate reviews of research, what sources for performance criteria does the teacher educator use? After reading the model proposals, we surmise that many of the performance criteria represent "expert opinion" derived from experience and from interpretations of the results of descriptive studies of classroom teaching.

Descriptive studies have been used to develop normative data on teaching as it occurs in typical classrooms. Using various observational category systems, investigators have concluded that there is very little difference in the interaction patterns which occur when teachers teach different subjects in elementary classrooms; that there is frequent use of teacher behaviors classified as "controlling"; and that a great deal of time is spent on managerial or administrative details (Furst and Amidon, 1967; Hughes, 1962; Perkins, 1964). Data from studies made of high school teaching show that teachers spend much of their time covering content that requires but one common pattern of student thinking—fact stating or cognitive memory. Furthermore, the research yields little evidence that teachers are concerned with any logical strategy of subject matter delineation (Bellack *et al.*, 1966; Gallagher and Aschner, 1963; Smith *et al.*, 1962, 1964, 1967).

The descriptive behavioral data obtained from these classroom studies is then compared with what the educators believe "should" occur in classrooms. The bases for these imperatives are seldom stated explicitly, but probably derive from several sources. Teacher training then becomes a procedure for closing the gap between the behaviors which *do* occur and the behaviors which educators believe *should* occur by training the teachers in the desired behaviors. For example, after viewing the data on teacher use of controlling behaviors, one researcher suggested that teachers learn to use "public criteria" and "open structure" in the classroom (Hughes, 1962). The finding that high school teachers exhibit high frequencies of cognitive memory (rote) episodes led one investigator to recommend that practice in the use of topics on higher cognitive levels be introduced to teachers (Gallagher, 1968).

THE LACK OF KNOWLEDGE Unfortunately, the relationship between the teacher behaviors advocated by educational experts and the consequent learning by students has not been thoroughly investigated. In addition, little investigation has been made of any differences in student product measures which occur *after* teachers have been trained in these missing performance criteria.

One unfortunate consequence of the lack of substantial research on the relationship between teacher behavior and student growth is the paradox of different institutions training teachers in opposite performance criteria. Thus, the Far West Regional Laboratory uses Minicourse I to train teachers to repeat student answers *less* often, while the Northwest Regional Laboratory has a training program in Flanders' Interaction Analysis which lists *more* teacher repetition of student answers as one measure of the preferred "indirect teaching."

Perhaps the beginning of wisdom in the study and improvement of teaching behavior is the confession of our lack of knowledge that can be applied with confidence to a teacher education program. Educational researchers have *not* provided those who train teachers with a repertoire of teaching skills which indicate to a teacher that if he increases behavior *X* and/or decreases behavior *Y* there will be a concomitant change in the cognitive or affective achievement of his students. It is time to stop touting structural panaceas and to begin developing the research which may produce the knowledge. We recommend that the research take place within the framework of the model programs.

Additional Sources of Hypotheses for Performance Criteria

An educator might search four areas of research for promising variables which could be incorporated into rigorous classroom experiments or be developed into performance criteria: laboratory studies, subject matter research, experimental classroom studies, and "process-product studies."

LABORATORY STUDIES Laboratory studies on meaningful human learning, in which the instruction is mediated by written materials, audiotapes, or films, appear in the learning sections of all educational psychology textbooks. Generalizations derived from this research are frequently developed as teacher competencies (e.g., use of reinforcement, spaced review, identification of major elements in a concept).

Readers of such reviews should be advised of the limited generalizability of these laboratory studies. The results of these studies seem to have little direct relevance to school learning because their research situation is so different from classroom instruction. For example, in laboratory studies the period of instruction is seldom longer than three hours; each subject studies individually, without group interaction; the treatments are usually highly structured; and the "teacher" is the experimenter or his assistant. Such constraints of design limit any generalization we might make from these studies to the *training of teachers* who will be interacting with their *classes.*

SUBJECT MATTER RESEARCH Another source of behaviors for instructional programs is the considerable research on instructional procedures within particular subject areas such as reading, arithmetic, spelling, science, and mathematics. Such research is regularly summarized in the *Review of Educational Research,* the *Encyclopedia of Educational Research,* the *Handbook of Research on Teaching,* and the major journals in each subject area.

One would think that such subject area research would have yielded evidence on the relationship among teacher behavior, instructional materials, and student performance. However, the *design* of this research frequently precludes direct applicability to teacher education programs. Many of these studies are conducted in classrooms where the instruction is mediated by a teacher, but in most cases only one or two classrooms receive the experimental treatment while one or two classrooms receive the contrast treatment, and the individual *student* is used as the sampling unit. In fact, the proper unit of analysis for generalizing to the training of teachers is the mean score of each *classroom* (Campbell and Stanley, 1963, p. 193; Walberg, 1970a, pp. 564–65).

Even when large-scale curriculum studies are conducted, the specific treatments are vaguely defined and rarely monitored (Katz, 1969; Welch, 1970). When observations are made of instruction within specific curriculum programs, investigators have noted significant variability of teacher behavior (Conners and Eisenberg, 1966; Gallagher, 1970). Such variability and lack of specificity indicate that in curriculum studies we have compared the effect of one vague complex of behaviors with the effect of another one (Travers, 1969). Because of these problems and others, a reviewer of classroom teaching of mathematics noted that, "Despite long and active interest in the problem, research offers few important guidelines in the search for personal attributes, classroom types, or educational preparation of successful teachers" (Fey, 1969, p. 535).

EXPERIMENTAL CLASSROOM STUDIES The best potential source of variables for teacher education programs is classroom experimental studies in which various instructional procedures are used and the effects of these different procedures on pupils are reported. In such studies the experimental teachers are trained to exhibit specific instructional behaviors, such as asking questions on a higher cognitive level (Rogers and Davis, 1970), using more praise and support of student ideas (Carline, 1969), or teaching a mathematics unit in specified ways (Worthen, 1968a,b). The contrast or control teachers either follow their normal, "natural" procedures or use a specified, alternative instructional procedure.

In order to furnish conclusions which can be applied to teacher education programs, we need studies in which (1) the teacher is the statistical unit of analysis; (2) teachers or classes are randomly assigned to treatment; (3) observational data are obtained on the fidelity of teacher behavior to the experimental or contrast treatment and on the behavior of the students, while similar observational data are obtained on events in the classrooms of teachers who follow their normal procedures; and (4) student performance is assessed by a variety of end-of-course tests. Such studies are rare. To date we have found no more than ten studies which satisfy all four criteria. The scarcity of such studies is not surprising because conducting them involves enormous problems of methodology, administration, and teacher training.

PROCESS-PRODUCT RESEARCH A fourth source of variables for teacher education programs is the process-product research. By process-product studies we mean investigations which attempt to relate observed teacher behaviors to student outcome measures (Mitzel, 1960). Such studies are best labeled as "correlational" because only naturally occurring behaviors are observed, although some investigators have used statistical procedures ordinarily associated with experiments to analyze their data.

In process-product studies the independent variables—the teacher behaviors—are recorded using observational category systems or rating systems. Category systems are classified as *low-inference* measures (Gage, 1969; Rosenshine, 1970c) because the items focus upon specific, denotable, relatively objective behaviors (e.g., teacher repetition of student ideas, teacher use of evaluative question), and because such events are recorded as frequency counts. Rating systems are classified as *high-inference* measures because the items on rating instruments (e.g., clarity, warmth, task-orientation, class cohesiveness) require that an observer infer these constructs from a series of events. In process-product studies the dependent variables are student performance measures, usually adjusted (by regression) for initial status.

The results of process-product studies must be treated with caution because these are correlational, not experimental, studies. The results of such studies can be deceptive in that they suggest causation although the teacher behaviors which are related to student achievement may be only minor indicators of a complex of behaviors that we have not yet identified.

REVIEW OF PROCESS-PRODUCT STUDIES

Process-product studies have produced some of the best variables on the relationship between teacher behavior and student achievement. Unlike the myriad competencies outlined by the model program builders, the skills listed below have some support in studies of naturally occurring teacher behavior and student achievement. The results of these studies provide hypotheses upon which to build teacher training models.

However, these are not variables which can be placed in teacher education programs with the assurance that training teachers in these behaviors will enhance student performance. Much more study is needed before these behaviors and their effects will be clarified. In particular, we will need studies in which teachers are trained to modify their behavior while the effects of these modifications upon student achievement are noted.

Most of the variables that have been consistently related to student achievement were derived from high-inference rating scales, which means that the teacher behaviors which comprise "clarity of persentation" or "enthusiasm," for example, have not been concretely specified. We hope researchers will seek the low-inference variables.

Some fifty process-product studies have been reported. In approximately forty of these studies classroom behavior was sampled during one or two school semesters; in ten of the studies the instructional period ranged from seven minutes to ten one-hour lessons. In all of the studies naturally occurring teacher behavior was observed, and in most of the studies the teacher was the sampling unit. The variables described below were abstracted from more detailed reviews (Rosenshine, 1970a,b) and are the most promising of the variables studied. The variables with the strongest support are presented first.

A number of limitations should be noted. First, all the studies were conducted in classrooms with normal children. Second, in most studies only the class mean was employed in the analyses, and few attempts were made to determine the relationships between teacher behavior and student achievement for subgroups of students differing in achievement, aptitude, or personality. Reports on these subgroups will not be reviewed in this chapter. Third, these studies have focused on *general* teaching behaviors which, hopefully, will be effective across all subject areas and types of curriculum, whereas in the original reviews, relationships between teacher behavior and student achievement were reported for each subject area. However, a study of the tables in the reviews shows that specific teacher behaviors were *not* more consistently related to student achievement in one subject area than in others. Finally, this review covers only the relationships between teacher behaviors and student achievement. Other important outcome variables, such as student attitudes toward self, school, and subject area, were not considered here because such outcome variables merit a separate review. Again, we caution the reader that this review is based on correlational, not experimental, studies.

A description of the eleven strongest variables contained in this research is presented below together with the results obtained when these variables were studied. The best results were obtained on the first five variables; the results were less conclusive on the last six variables. The major focus is upon process-product studies, but experimental classroom studies are cited whenever appropriate.

1. Clarity[1]

The cognitive clarity of a teacher's presentation has been studied in seven investigations in which student or observer ratings were used. The investigators used different descriptions of clarity:

1. "Clarity of presentation" (Belgard, Rosenshine, and Gage, 1968; Fortune, 1967; Fortune, Gage and Shutes, 1966);
2. whether "the points the teacher made were clear and easy to understand" (Solomon, Bezdek, and Rosenberg, 1963);
3. whether "the teacher was able to explain concepts clearly . . . had facility with her material and enough background to answer her children's questions intelligently" (Wallen, 1966, 1st grade; Wallen, 1966, 3rd grade);
4. whether the cognitive level of the teacher's lesson appeared to be "just right most of the time" (Chall and Feldmann, 1966).

Significant results on at least one criterion measure were obtained in all seven studies. In those studies for which simple correlations were available, the significant correlations ranged from .37 to .71.

Unfortunately, we are unclear as to the low-inference behaviors which comprise clarity. In studies employing low-inference behaviors, investigators found that the most effective teachers (1) spent less time answering student questions which require interpretation of what the teacher said (Solomon, Bezdek, and Rosenberg, 1963); (2) phrased questions so that they were answered the first time without additional information or additional questions interspersed before the student responded (Wright and Nuthall, 1970); or (3) used fewer "vagueness words" such as "some," "many,"' "of course," and "a little" (Hiller, Fisher, and Kaess, 1969). Future research might be directed at determining those low-inference behaviors whose frequency of occurrence is highly correlated with ratings on clarity. Once these behaviors are identified, they can be taught in a teacher education program, and the effects of teacher use of the behaviors on student achievement can be assessed.

Another high-inference variable, namely *organization*, may be similar to clarity because in the study by Solomon, Bezdek, and Rosenberg (1963), student and observer ratings on "clarity of the lesson," "coherence of the lesson," and "organization of the lesson" all loaded on the same significant factor. The organization of the lesson has also been studied using observer or student ratings on the item "organization of the lesson" (Belgard, Rosenshine, and

[1] The reader should note that all of the studies cited below employed a number of variables as independent measures, and the results of these studies appear in more than one place. For example, one study of first-grade instruction (Wallen, 1966, 1st grade) appears below under the review of "clarity," and also under "task orientation," because both variables were significant in that study.

Gage, 1968; Fortune, 1967; Fortune, Gage, and Shutes, 1966), and student ratings on seven item scales which included items such as, "There is a great deal of confusion during class meetings" (Anderson and Walberg, 1968; Walberg and Anderson, 1968; Walberg, 1969).

Positive relationships between ratings on the behavior labeled "organization" and regression-adjusted student achievement scores were obtained in all the studies mentioned above. Significant correlations between ratings on organization and at least one student achievement measure were obtained in four of six independent studies (Anderson and Walberg, 1968; Belgard, Rosenshine, and Gage, 1968; Fortune, 1967; Solomon, Bezdek, and Rosenberg, 1963). The significant correlations ranged from .34 to .67.

Future research will be necessary to determine the specific behaviors which comprise "clarity" or the training procedures which are most likely to achieve high ratings on the clarity of their presentation.

2. *Variability*

A number of studies focused on the teacher's use of variety or variability during the lesson. One investigator (Anthony, 1967) counted the variety of instructional materials, types of tests, and types of teaching devices used by the teacher. Another investigator (Lea, 1964) asked teachers to mark daily checklists on the number of different activities and materials used during social studies lessons. In two studies the investigators coded the cognitive level of classroom discourse and expressed these frequency counts as ratios so that the teacher who employed more cognitive variation in the discourse received higher scores (Furst, 1967; Thompson and Bowers, 1968). Significant results favoring variability were obtained on at least one criterion measure in all four studies.

Other investigators asked students or observers to mark rating scales on (1) the teacher's flexibility in procedure (Solomon, Bezdek, and Rosenberg, 1963), (2) whether the teacher was "adaptable" or "inflexible" (Fortune, 1967), and (3) the amount of extra equipment, books, displays, resource materials, and student activities (Torrance and Parent, 1966; Walberg, 1969). Significant results relating flexibility or abundance of materials to at least one measure of student achievement were obtained in all four studies. In the studies for which simple correlations were available, the correlations ranged from .24 to .54.

Both high-inference and low-inference correlational studies have indicated that student achievement is positively related to classrooms where a variety of instructional procedures and materials is provided, and where the teacher varies the cognitive level of discourse and of student tasks. It seems worthwhile to study experimentally the effects of training teachers to use this variety.

A variable such as variety appears to be distinct from "flexibility" as defined in recent studies. Flexibility has been studied by counting *any* form of variation in teacher behavior. For example, Soar (1966) defined flexibility as the number of cells in an Interaction Analysis matrix necessary to account for 60 percent of the tallies. A teacher who used a large number of different cells in the one-hundred-cell matrix would have a high flexibility score. Of eight studies of flexibility, *none* yielded significant results (Flanders, 1970, 2nd grade, 4th grade, 6th grade, 7th grade, 8th grade; Snider, 1966; Soar, 1966; Vorreyer, 1965). In contrast, in studies of variability, changes of particular kinds, rather than just any change, were noted.

3. *Enthusiasm*

Teacher enthusiasm has been assessed by:

1. Observer ratings on paired adjectives such as "stimulating vs. dull," "original vs. stereotyped," or "alert vs. apathetic" (Fortune, 1967; Kleinman, 1964; Wallen, 1966).
2. Observer estimation of the amount of vigor and power exhibited by the teacher during classroom presentation (Solomon, Bezdek, and Rosenberg, 1963).
3. Student ratings on the teacher's involvement, excitement, or interest regarding his subject matter (Solomon, Bezdek, and Rosenberg, 1963).

Significant results relating enthusiasm to student achievement on at least one criterion measure were obtained in all five studies in which the variable was studied ($rs = .36$ to $.62$), and all nonsignificant results were in a positive direction ($rs = .10$ to $.30$) (Fortune, 1966; Kleinman, 1964; Solomon, Bezdek, and Rosenberg, 1963; Wallen, 1966, 1st and 3rd grades).

Although the specific low-inference behaviors which comprise enthusiasm have not yet been identified, the results from correlational and experimental studies suggest that movement, gesture, and voice inflections comprise at least part of this variable (see Rosenshine, 1970d). There is also a hint that mixtures of teacher questions, especially the use of questions calling for interpretation of facts, may be part of the constellation perceived as enthusiasm. New studies should be conducted to determine the low-inference behaviors which comprise enthusiasm.

It may be possible, however, to train teachers to be more enthusiastic even if we do not know the low-inference behaviors involved. In an experimental study (Mastin, 1963) twenty teachers were given identical materials and told to teach one lesson with enthusiasm and the other without enthusiasm. According to the report, the teachers did not receive further training. The student scores on posttests following these lessons consistently and significantly favored the lessons taught with enthusiasm. Unfortunately, there was no observation of the teachers' classroom behavior.

4. *Task-Oriented and/or Businesslike Behaviors*

In seven investigations, rating scales were used to estimate the degree to which a teacher was task-oriented, achievement-oriented, and/or businesslike. Unfortunately, the combination of these studies under one label is hazardous because there is no way to determine whether the different rating scales used can be combined under one category labeled "task-oriented and/or businesslike."

In two studies the investigators asked observers to rate the teachers using the paired adjectives which Ryans (1960) identified as comprising "Pattern Y: Businesslike"—evading-responsible, erratic-steady, disorganized-systematic, excitable-poised (Fortune, 1967; Kleinman, 1964). In another study (Chall and Feldmann, 1966) the teachers of high-achieving classes were rated by observers as emphasizing the stimulation of thought rather than information and skills. In two studies (Wallen, 1966, 1st grade and 3rd grade) "achievement-oriented teachers" were rated as being concerned that students learn something rather than that students enjoy themselves. In the sixth study students rated their teacher on the extent to which the teacher encouraged the class to work hard and to do independent and creative work (Torrance and Parent, 1966).

Significant results on at least one criterion measure were obtained in all six of the above studies (*rs* = .42 to .61). In the single study which yielded nonsignificant results (Beiderman, 1964), student ratings on "task-oriented" behavior were not analyzed separately but were combined with student ratings on the teacher's "teacher-centered" or "pupil-centered" behavior.

Ratings on task orientation may be a significant correlate of student achievement because "you get what you teach for." That is, those teachers who focused upon the learning of cognitive tasks obtained the highest student achievement in this area; those teachers who focused on other activities in the hope that cognitive growth would be obtained indirectly were less successful. The above extrapolation could be tested by using category systems to determine whether the teachers who are rated high in task orientation also spend more class time on cognitive tasks and/or use more cognitive reinforcers with their students.

It may be possible to train teachers to be more task-oriented without knowing the low-inference behaviors which comprise this variable. In one experiment (Wittrock, 1962) one group of student teachers was told that their grade in an educational psychology course would be based upon the gain their students attained in American history as compared to the gain attained by classroom students of the control student teachers. On a standardized achievement test the students of the experimental teachers achieved significantly superior growth to that of the students of the control teachers. Unfortunately, no observations were made of the classroom behaviors of the teachers in this experiment.

5. *Student Opportunity to Learn Criterion Material*

A major question in research of this type is whether the criterion instrument was relevant to the instruction. When the students are given a standardized pretest and posttest on reading, and the behaviors of the teacher are correlated with adjusted gain scores, the investigators seldom know whether the material on the posttest was indeed covered in the lessons.

In three investigations an attempt was made to assess the relationship between the material covered in the class and the class criterion score. Two investigators (Rosenshine, 1968b; Shutes, 1969) inspected typescripts of fifteen-minute lessons to determine the extent to which the material required to answer the posttest was covered in the lesson. A third investigator related the amount of time spent on various topics within four hour-long lessons to student achievement on these topics (Bellack *et al.,* 1966). In a cross-cultural study involving over 300,000 students in twelve countries, the teachers were shown the criterion test and were asked to rate whether "all or most (at least 75 percent)," "some (25 percent to 75 percent)," or "few (less than 25 percent)" of their students had had the opportunity to learn the *type* of problem exemplified by each test item (Husen, 1967).

Significant correlations between "opportunity to learn" and student achievement were obtained in three of the four studies (Husen, 1967; Rosenshine, 1968; Shutes, 1969) (*rs* = .16 to .40). The significant correlations in the cross-cultural study were obtained for each of four groups of students and represent the median within country correlation (Husen, 1967). That significant results did not occur in the fourth study (Bellack *et al.,* 1966) may have been because the test *items* themselves were not studied.

Overall, the correlations between measures of opportunity to learn and student achievement are positive, significant, and consistent. Note that in the largest of these studies (Husen, 1967), the teachers had never seen the test material before and were asked whether students had had an opportunity to learn material *of this type.* These results suggest that there is a positive correlation between the types of *cognitive processes* the students had an opportunity to learn and student performance on the international mathematics test. (However, the correlations are based on teacher reports and must be corroborated by direct observation.) One implication for teacher education is that it is important to orient teachers toward cognitive classroom activities if we wish to enhance student cognitive growth. Experimental studies that test these ideas would be desirable.

The high, significant correlations obtained in two other studies discussed above (Rosenshine, 1968b; Shutes, 1969) can be interpreted as measuring the degree to which teachers trained their students on the criterion items. Such results have implications for the statistical analyses of studies of teaching and will be discussed in the next section.

6. *Use of Student Ideas and General Indirectness*

The behavior identified as "teacher use of student ideas" was originally developed by Flanders (1965) and appears as Category 3 of his Interaction Analysis (IA) system. Although considerable correlational and descriptive research has been conducted using IA, the variable "use of student ideas" remains ambiguous. Flanders (1970) has attempted to solve the problems of definition by dividing this category into five subcategories of behaviors:

1. *Acknowledging* the student's idea by repeating the nouns and logical connectives he has expressed;
2. *Modifying* the idea by rephrasing it or conceptualizing it in the teacher's own words;
3. *Applying* the idea by using it to reach an inference or take the next step in a logical analysis of a problem;
4. *Comparing* the idea by drawing a relationship between it and ideas expressed earlier by the students or the teacher;
5. *Summarizing* what was said by an individual student or group of students.

Flanders reported (personal communication) that at least 60 percent of the behaviors classified as Category 3 consist of simple repetition by the teacher of what the student said.

Eight studies have been found in which counts of total use of student ideas and/or counts of extended (more than three seconds) use of student ideas were correlated with measures of student achievement. A significant bivariate correlation between teacher use of student ideas and student achievement was *not* obtained in any study. However, in seven of the eight studies correlations were positive (Flanders, 1970, 4th grade, 6th grade, 7th grade, 8th grade; Perkins, 1965; Soar, 1966; Wright and Nuthall, 1970) (*rs* = .17 to .40). The consistency of these results suggest that the variable "teacher use of student ideas" appears important enough to warrant more intensive study.

Another variable derived from the Flanders' Interaction Analysis matrix has been labeled "indirectness." It consists of the combined frequencies of teacher behaviors labeled (1) acceptance of student feeling, (2) praise or encouragement, and (3) use of student ideas. Such behaviors may be similar to the variable labeled "emotional climate" (Medley and Mitzel, 1959).

The results of six studies utilizing this variable were similar to those obtained when "teacher use of student ideas" was studied. Significant results were obtained in one study (Flanders, 1970, 6th grade), although positive correlations were obtained in four of the five remaining studies (Flanders, 1970, 4th grade, 7th grade, 8th grade; Medley and Mitzel, 1959) (*rs* = .12 to .41). Because the variable "teacher use of student ideas" is part of the more general variable "indirectness," both variables appear to be useful for future research.

A third variable, the ratio of "indirect" to "direct" behaviors, also appears to be useful for future study. This ratio has been significantly related to student achievement in only one study (LaShier, 1967), but positive correlations were obtained in eleven of thirteen investigations (*rs* = .12 to .41).

There have been four experimental classroom studies in which teachers were trained to be more supportive, their classroom behaviors were observed, and class achievement scores were compared with those obtained in classrooms which received a contrast or control treatment. Unfortunately, the results were not statistically significant, nor was there a discernible trend in the four studies (Carline, 1969; Gunnison, 1968; Herman *et al.*, 1969; Miller, 1966).

7. *Criticism*

Teacher use of behaviors labeled "criticism" or "control" has been one of the most frequently counted variables in process-product research. Seventeen studies were reported in which observers counted these behaviors. Many of the investigators used more than one measure of criticism. For example, in five separate studies one investigator computed counts of (1) total teacher use of criticism and giving of directions, (2) extended (more than three seconds in duration) teacher criticism and giving of directons, and (3) teacher criticism or directions in response to student comments (Flanders, 1970). Another investigator (Hunter, 1968) developed separate categories for hostile or strong disapproval, neutral or mild disapproval, directive statements related to school, and teacher justification of authority. Other investigators (Harris and Serwer, 1966; Harris *et al.*, 1968) divided teacher criticism into negative motivation and control.

Significant negative relationships between some form of criticism and at least one criterion measure were obtained in six of seventeen studies (Anthony, 1967; Flanders, 1970, 7th grade; Harris *et al.*, 1968; Hunter, 1968; Soar, 1966; Wallen, 1966, 1st grade) (*rs* = −.38 to −.61). Both positive and negative relationships were obtained in two studies which employed factor analysis (Perkins, 1965; Spaulding, 1965), and significantly positive results were obtained in one study (Harris and Serwer, 1966) (*rs* = .28 to .29). On the whole, there is a trend for significant negative relationships between teacher criticism and student achievement, but the results are not as strong as some of the other variables discussed in this paper.

If only the direction of the correlation is considered, negative correlations between all observed measures of criticism and all measures of achievement were obtained in twelve of the seventeen studies (Anthony, 1967; Cook, 1967; Flanders, 1970, 4th grade, 6th grade, 7th grade, 8th grade; Harris *et al.*, 1968; Hunter, 1968; Soar, 1966; Wallen, 1966, 1st grade, 3rd grade; Wright and Nuthall, 1970). These correlations ranged from —.04 to —.62. Positive correlations between all measures of criticism and all measures of achievement were obtained in two studies (Harris and Serwer, 1966; Morsh, 1956), but these correlations tended to be small (*r*s from .05 to .29). *Both* positive *and* negative relationships between criticism and achievement were obtained in three of the seventeen studies (Flanders, 1970, 2nd grade; Perkins, 1965; Spaulding, 1965). In sum, the *direction* of the correlations shows a strong trend for a negative relationship between criticism and student achievement.

In sixteen of the studies it is possible to compare the relationships of different types or intensities of criticism to student achievement. For example, the results on "mild disapproval" can be compared with those on "strong disapproval" (Hunter, 1968), or the results on "rejecting a student response" can be compared with "teacher criticizes or justifies authority" (Perkins, 1965). In ten of the seventeen studies, the stronger form of criticism had a higher negative correlation with achievement than the milder form. Thus, teachers who use extreme amounts or forms of criticism usually have classes which achieve less in most subject areas.

In no study was there a significant negative correlation between mild forms of criticism or control and student achievement. Such mild forms include telling a student that his answer was incorrect or providing academic directions. Thus there is no evidence to support a claim that teachers should avoid telling a student he was wrong or should avoid giving academic directions.

Variables such as teacher use of differing forms of approval and disapproval are frequently used as performance criteria in teacher education programs. But it is impossible to make any specific recommendations on the implications of this research for teacher training for two reasons. First, in correlational studies such as these we do not know if the teacher's use of criticism is self-initiated, results from the characteristics of the students, or results from an interaction of the teacher and students. Second, we do not know if the variables labeled as approval or disapproval in one study are comparable with those so labeled in another. In future research there is a need to subdivide these variables into smaller units, such as increasing levels of affect, and to design observational systems that enable us to record the context in which these behaviors occur.

8. *Use of Structuring Comments*

Investigators who have counted the use of teacher "structuring" statements generally refer to statements designed to provide an overview or a cognitive scaffolding for what is to happen or has happened. Such statements have been identified at the start and at the end of lessons and at the start and end of sections of lessons. Teacher statements which precede a question, statements which summarize an interchange, the use of a clear signal to indicate when one part of a lesson ends and another begins, and verbal markers of importance (e.g., "Now get this") are among the diverse procedures used to identify structuring. Teacher structuring statements have been *counted* in four investigations, and significant results were obtained in all four (Furst, 1967; Penny, 1969; Soar, 1966; Wright and Nuthall, 1970). Structuring statements were also cited in two investigations in which the significance levels were not given (Crossman and Olson, 1969; Fortune, 1967). Although each investigator gave fairly precise operational definitions of the variable, the category systems used were so different that we cannot make comparisons of the results.

In three studies in which raters estimated the adequacy of the beginning or the ending of the lesson, there were significant correlations (*r*s = .35 to .69) between ratings for *either* the beginning *or* the end of the lesson and the criterion measure (Belgard, Rosenshine, and Gage, 1968; Fortune, 1967; Fortune, Gage, and Shutes, 1966). Although all correlations were positive, the correlations were significant for both the beginning and the end of the lesson in only one study (Fortune, 1967). Unfortunately, we are unable to determine whether there is any relationship between the ratings given to the beginning or end of the lesson and the various counts of structuring.

The results to date indicate that the various forms of structuring merit further study, but it is impossible to synthesize the results in a manner which can be translated into teaching competencies. Only fragmentary hints for teacher training programs can be offered—such as considering providing a moderate number of statements before asking a question, reviewing at the end of a series of interchanges, using a review at the start or end of a lesson, or providing clear signals as to when one part of a lesson ends and another begins.

9. *Types of Questions*

TWO CLASSIFICATIONS Several investigators have studied the relationship between teacher use of various types of questions (or varied types of classroom discourse) and student achievement. Most investigators have used a scheme in which questions are classified into two forms. In general, the two forms might be labeled "lower cognitive level" and "higher cognitive level" questions, although few investigators used these specific labels. Each investigator provided fairly clear definitions of his categories, and most investigators tended to classify questions that focused on "what" or "where" as lower-level questions and questions that focused on "why" and "how" as higher-level questions. However, classifications among investigators overlap in such a way that a question classified as lower-level in one investigation might have been classified as higher-level in another.

Of the seven investigations in which questions were classified into two types, significant results were *not* obtained in four (Harris and Serwer, 1966; Harris *et al.*, 1968; Perkins, 1965; Wright and Nuthall, 1970). The reports did not present sufficient detail to specify the over-all direction of the correlations. Of the three investigations in which significant results were reported, the high-achieving teachers asked *more* "high-level" questions in one study (Kleinman, 1964), but asked *fewer* "open-ended" questions in another study (Spaulding, 1965). In the third study, the highest achieving teachers were those who mixed convergent and divergent questions (Thompson and Bowers, 1968).

Thus, the classification of all questions into only two forms has not yielded consistent significant results or any discernible trend.

MULTIPLE CLASSIFICATIONS OF DISCOURSE Only two studies were found which used multiple classifications of teacher questions or types of teacher-student discourse. Significant results were obtained in both (Conners and Eisenberg, 1966; Solomon, Bezdek, and Rosenberg, 1963). The studies are not easily compared because they differed widely in design, coding procedures, and focus. Not even a tentative conclusion can be drawn about the relationship between various cognitive levels of discourse and student achievement. The most useful conclusion at this point is that classification of questions and/or types of discourse into three or more types appears to offer greater potential for future research than the use of only two classifications.

10. Probing

The variable "probing" generally refers to teacher responses to student answers which encourage the student (or another student) to elaborate upon his answer. In one investigation the teacher "elicited clarification in a non-threatening way" (Spaulding, 1965), and in another (Soar, 1966), teachers were scored as encouraging "interpretation, generalization, and solution" if they asked such a question *or* if they responded to a student in such a manner. In a third investigation (Wright and Nuthall, 1970), various types of teacher responses were counted, such as redirection of the question to another student, or the asking of another question to the student who first answered. Significant results were obtained in all three studies (rs = .29 to .54), but the variety of methods used to record such behavior precluded any synthesis of the results. We can conclude only that further study of such teacher behaviors appears warranted.

11. Level of Difficulty of Instruction

Student perceptions of the difficulty of the instruction have been assessed in four studies through student questionnaires. One investigator (Walberg, 1969) used a seven item scale which contained items such as "The class is best suited for the smartest students." However, two of the items in the difficulty scale may refer to the aptitude or brightness of the students in the class: "Students in the class tend to be much brighter than those in the rest of the school"; "Many students in the school would have difficulty doing the advanced work of the class." Because the challenge of the course and the brightness of the students are both in the same scale, it is impossible to determine from the data whether the measured student perception of "difficulty" is a function of the teacher's approach, the ability of the class, or an interaction of the two.

In the international study cited above (Husen, 1967), students were asked to rate the difficulty of learning mathematics on a five point scale. In the third study (Nikoloff, 1965) a specially prepared questionnaire was developed to assess how strict the teacher was in demanding high standards in English composition. In the fourth study (Torrance and Parent, 1966) one of the questionnaire items was: "This class is one of the hardest in the school."

There was a clear, significant relationship between student perception of difficulty and student achievement in two of the four studies (Torrance and Parent, 1966; Walberg, 1969), and no discernible trend in the other two studies (Husen, 1967; Nikoloff, 1965).

Student perception of level of difficulty appears to be a fascinating area for future study because in two studies perceptions of difficulty were *positively* related to achievement. However, the issue is more complex because in the study with the strongest results (Walberg, 1969) *mean* perceptions of difficulty in this special physics program were *lower* than perceptions of difficulty of the regular physics program.

Summary of Process-Product Results

SUMMARY OF STRONGEST FINDINGS Of all the variables which have been investigated in process-product studies to date, five variables have strong support from correlational studies and six variables have less support but appear to deserve future study. The five variables which yielded the strongest relationships with measures of student achievement are: clarity, variability, enthusiasm, task orientation and/or businesslike behavior, and student opportunity to learn. The six less strong variables are: use of student ideas and/or teacher indirectness, use of criticism, use of structuring comments, use of multiple levels of discourse, probing, and perceived difficulty of the course.

The relationships are positive for ten of the variables and negative for use of criticism.

SUMMARY OF NONSIGNIFICANT RESULTS At first glance, the above list of the strongest findings may appear to represent mere educational platitudes. Their value can be appreciated, however, only when they are compared to the behavioral characteristics, equally virtuous and "obvious," which have *not* shown significant or consistent relationships with achievement *to date*. These variables, which are taken from the larger reviews (Rosenshine, 1970a,b), are listed below, and the method by which they were assessed follows in parenthesis: nonverbal approval (counting), praise (counting), warmth (rating), ratio of all indirect behaviors to all direct teacher behaviors, or the *i/d* ratio (counting), flexibility (counting), questions or interchanges classified into two types (counting), teacher talk (counting), student talk (counting), student participation (rating), number of teacher-student interactions (counting), student absence, teacher absence, teacher time spent on class participation (rating), teacher experience, and teacher knowledge of subject area. It is possible that future studies employing improved designs and improved analyses of the data, or future reviews of the same literature may yield somewhat different conclusions. However, such caution works both ways—one cannot claim that the above nonsignificant variables are correlates of student achievement until he can marshal supportive data.

FUTURE RESEARCH ON TEACHER BEHAVIORS

This final section includes a number of suggestions for future research on teacher behaviors, although the suggestions are not exhaustive. The major section is on future process-product studies because of the importance which many researchers and educators give to knowledge developed in such settings. Many of the ideas for improved process-product research also apply to the development of experimental classroom studies, an area which has been badly neglected. Finally, we shall discuss how process-product and experimental studies could be conducted within the context of the model teacher education programs, and we shall emphasize the importance of such research as part of the evaluation of these programs.

Future Process-Product Research

Currently, our view of the state of the art of process-product research on teaching is both promising and discouraging. We note that the early expectations that the counting of relatively objective teaching behaviors would yield consistent, significant correlations with student achievement certainly have not yet been fulfilled. Indeed, the most promising results have been obtained in studies in which teacher behavior was described using rating scales. The results obtained through the use of ratings on such variables as clarity, enthusiasm, task orientation, and variation appear very promising.

After ten years of process-product research, fifty studies, and mixed results, some researchers would claim that such correlational research will not be productive in the future. Because of the limited research, and because of the methodological problems which may exist in most of these studies, any judgment on the worth of this research would be premature. However, before any conclusion is reached, we believe that there should be at least a second generation of this research incorporating some of the suggestions we present below. These suggestions cover four major areas: selection of variables, procedures for coding classroom events, administrative design of the studies, and statistical procedures for analyzing the results. Some topics discussed in each of these areas seem to be applicable to more than one area.

Selection of Variables

We offer four suggestions for the selection of variables in future process-product studies: (1) the use of variables available in existing observational category systems and rating systems; (2) the use of a greater variety of variables, such as more comprehensive cognitive variables—e.g., multiple classification of questions, use of varied activities, and similar variables cited earlier in this review; (3) the use of more variables developed from laboratory studies; and (4) the use of high-inference and low-inference variables together in the same investigation.

VARIABLES FROM EXISTING OBSERVATIONAL SYSTEMS At least four hundred observational category systems and rating systems have been developed, and although many of the variables overlap or are duplicated in different systems, a large pool of distinct variables has been developed. However, most of the new observational category systems have been used to *describe* teaching; fewer than fifteen have been used to relate classroom behaviors to student growth. Similarly, most of the rating systems have been used to *judge* the quality of teaching without determining the relationship between or among specific variables and student growth. It is particularly unfortunate that so few of the observational systems have been used in process-product studies. Many of the developers have spent a great deal of time developing specific denotable variables which can become promising concepts for improving teaching. Yet few people have attempted to determine which of these hundreds of concepts are worth using and studying.

USING MORE VARIABLES FROM LABORATORY RESEARCH There has been considerable study in laboratory-type settings of meaningful human learning and the effect of different types of instructional materials upon achievement. But there is little overlap between the variables developed for use in classroom observational studies and the variables being investigated in laboratory and curriculum material research. For example, in one review of specific treatment variables associated with curriculum materials (Popham, 1969), the major headings were: organizers, relevant practice, knowledge of results, promoting learner interest, prompting, sequencing, and pacing. An anthology of research reports on meaningful human learning (Anderson *et al.*, 1969) included the following titles as section headings: "prompting and fading techniques," "the student response," "reinforcement and feedback," "facilitation of concept learning," and "organization and sequence." In our review of process-product studies we referred to variables such as "enthusiasm," "variation," and "indirectness."

This lack of common variables between laboratory and classroom research may occur because studies of "instruction" have focused on instruction mediated by a teacher. In effect, two separate disciplines are being developed to study meaningful human learning. One contains a minimum and the other a maximum of verbal interaction. Although there is some overlap between the two disciplines in areas such as reinforcement and feedback, there has been little attempt to assimilate one with the other. Occasionally bridges are built. Nuthall (1968) used programmed materials to investigate the effects of classroom instructional strategies identified by Smith, Meux, *et al.* (1967), and the study by Worthen (1968a,b) was explicitly designed to test whether the laboratory studies on discovery learning could be replicated in a natural classroom setting. We hope that more such interaction will develop, and that variables developed in the laboratory will be applied to classroom research and vice versa. For example, we should hope that many of the ideas on "testlike events" or "learning to learn" could be applied to correlational and experimental classroom research.

NONAFFECTIVE VARIABLES One conclusion which can be reached from the process-product research summarized here is that some of the cognitive and nonaffective variables seem to be excellent predictors of student achievement. However, affective variables have been studied much more frequently in process-product studies. More research on nonaffective variables seems warranted. Promising but insufficiently researched variables include multiple classification of questions, probing responses to student answers, variation of activities and the cognitive level of the discourse, and use of structuring statements.

EMPLOYING HIGH-INFERENCE AND LOW-INFERENCE MEASURES Throughout the foregoing review of research we have noted that we could not specify the low-inference measures which comprise the behaviors most closely related to nonaffective areas, such as "clarity," "task orientation," or "enthusiasm." Yet such high-inference items have greater predictive validity than most of the low-inference items. Perhaps one reason for this lack of specificity is that investigators have seldom used *both* high-inference and low-inference measures in the same study, or they have not attempted to determine the specific behaviors which comprise a high rating on "clarity" or "enthusiasm."

The use of both high-inference and low-inference measures in future studies may be most advantageous. Rating scales may allow a student or an observer to process a large number of cues before he makes a decision on a teacher's "task-oriented" behavior, whereas someone using an observational category system is unable to perform such processing because of the nature of the system. At the same time, the low-inference measures can provide specific details on "task-oriented" behavior which might escape an investigator limited to high-inference measures.

One procedure for combining the two observational procedures would be to use student questionnaires to describe the high-inference behaviors and outside observers and recodings to describe the low-inference behaviors.

Modifications in Coding Procedures

Now that classroom observational category systems have been extensively used for more than twenty years, we should like to suggest some issues for readers to consider when using, modifying, and developing category systems.

NORMATIVE DATA AND INTER-INVESTIGATION RELIABILITY Anyone who uses an observational category system soon learns that the coding instructions supplied by the author usually are not sufficient to code the events which occur in a classroom. Inevitably, users are required to make additional ground rules, or coding instructions, to cover the unforeseen behaviors. Different investigators who have used the same category system (such as Interaction Analysis) may have created quite different ground rules.

As a result of these necessary modifications, it is difficult to obtain any normative data on classroom behavior. If five investigators who used the same observational system observed math instruction in different fifth-grade classrooms and obtained different descriptive data, we cannot know whether these differences reflected actual differences in behavior or differences in the ground rules developed by each team of investigators.

CODING CONCURRENT EVENTS The difficulty of including all concurrent events in a category system is illustrated by the category systems developed by Bellack and his associates (1966). In their study, *separate* analyses were made of the type of pedagogical moves (e.g., teacher solicits, student responds), the thought process occurring (e.g., explaining, evaluating), and the substantive area of the materials being studied.

Several recent modifications in category systems make the inclusion of concurrent events possible. One investigator (Gallagher, 1968) developed a category system in which each "topic" of classroom interaction is coded on three dimensions: instructional intent (content or skill), level of conceptualization (data, concept, or generalization), and style (description, expansion, or evaluation). Another investigator (Flanders, 1970) referred to a similar procedure as "multiple coding," and proposed that three or more numbers be entered as the coding of an event, and that these numbers represent various affective and cognitive activities. The advantage of such new coding procedures is that they provide us with more information on the context of classroom events, such as types of questions or types of teacher responses.

SEQUENCING In current process-product research, little attention has been given to the sequencing of events. For example, although investigators have counted the frequency of teacher behaviors categorized as rewarding and punishing, little attention has been paid to specifying the event which was rewarded or punished. Similarly, little distinction has been made between the use of structuring statements at the start of a series of lessons and the use of structuring statements within a lesson. Investigators have tended to use only the total frequency of structuring statements in their statistical analyses. In a similar vein, no one has investigated the effective difference between asking a broad question at the start of a lesson and asking a broad question at the end of a lesson. The suggestion that contextual behaviors and the sequencing of behaviors be considered implies that it may be fruitful to study teaching as a *strategy*. But although terms such as teaching strategy and teaching style are commonly used, investigators have not yet been able to define these terms using specific, denotable behaviors.

CODING OTHER CLASSROOM EVENTS More complex category systems can also provide for increased coding of gross classroom events. Some existing category systems make distinctions between discussion and laboratory periods, but further subdivisions within these categories are rarely made. Current observation instruments totally disregard the materials being read, the assignments students write, the use which the teacher makes of written or oral material, and the physical features of the room, such as seating arrangements and lighting.

SCOPE OF INDIVIDUAL CATEGORIES An emerging problem in the use of category systems is the optimal scope of each category, considering the fact that each category encompasses many behaviors. For example, the ten category system developed by Flanders (1965) is very easy to teach and to use, but many users complain that ten categories are too few. Such users believe that a teacher's use of academic directions should be coded differently from a teacher's use of disciplinary directions to a student; that a teacher's summary of a student's contribution should be coded differently from simple repetition of what a student said.

Users' requests for greater specificity have led some investigators (e.g., Amidon, Amidon, and Rosenshine, 1969; Flanders, 1970) to expand category systems through the use of subscripts for each category. The use of subscripts raises the question of the *optimal* size of these smaller units. It is possible to identify ten forms of "silence or confusion," or ten types of questions, but we do not know whether the results would be worth the extra work. Empirical study of the advantage of increasing the number of subscripts is difficult because the number of subscripts which can be created far exceeds the number of teachers in the usual sample studied in process-product studies.

ANALYTIC UNITS Early investigators have coded classroom events according to their duration. The Flanders Interaction Analysis System with its "three second rule" is an example of the use of time as the primary analytic unit. Other investigators have attempted to develop cognitive units under which the frequency of events is recorded. These investigators have developed complex units such as a "move" (Bellack *et al.,* 1966), a "venture" (Smith *et al.,* 1966), or a "topic" (Gallagher, 1968). These new analytic units are then coded as to their dominant cognitive process, the types of questions which occur within them, or teacher affective behavior. Although analytic units such as these are difficult to use, it does not follow automatically that other units which are easier to use—such as time or lines on a transcript—should be substituted for them. Whether a cognitive unit, a time unit, or a combination of the two is most appropriate for studying classroom interaction is an empirical question which has received too little study. We hope that the question of the appropriate analytic unit will be studied in the second generation of observational classroom studies.

Design of Process-Product Studies

Given a set of variables to represent important aspects of classroom instruction, and given a set of procedures to record the frequency, context, and sequence of these behaviors, the next problem is the design of an appropriate means to relate the observed behavior to the measured outcome.

The most frequently used design is one in which a pretest (or pretests) is given at the start of the semester, teacher and student behavior is sampled during a school year, and a posttest is administered at the end of the year. Such "long-term" studies have been criticized because in such situations there may not be an appropriate match among the curriculum materials, the teacher's aims and behaviors, and the criterion instruments. For instance, G. Nuthall (personal communication) has asked this question: if one group of teachers is teaching skills *A, B,* and *C* very well, and another group is teaching skills *D, E,* and *F* very poorly, what will be shown if their classes are tested on skills *X, Y,* and *Z*?

Such criticism is particularly cogent if standardized achievement tests are used as criterion measures (Flanders, 1970). Such tests may be inappropriate measures of the influence of the teacher's behavior if the items on the tests are not relevant to the materials or skills taught in the classroom. Teachers may not be interested in standardized achievement tests (Jackson, 1968).

In many studies these tests may measure the aptitude of the learner or the pressure for academic achievement in the home rather than the influence of the teacher.

Currently we may be faced with the problem of teachers who are teaching for various goals, none or few of which may be related to the criterion test, while researchers are trying to see which teacher behaviors are related to goals that neither the teacher nor the students may perceive. However, it is possible to devise alternative designs in which the curriculum, the teacher's behaviors, and the criterion instruments are more closely related. These new designs, to be discussed below, focus on increasing the investigator's control over the teaching situation. The paradox is that the new situation may not represent naturally occurring teaching as it presently exists. Given the diverse goals of teachers, curriculum developers, students, and test developers, we question whether adequate designs can be developed to study the relationship between teacher behavior and student achievement in the typical, uncontrolled situation.

POSSIBLE MODIFICATIONS IN DESIGN Some of the above problems might be alleviated if we study teacher behavior over a shorter period of time, such as instructional periods ranging from fifteen minutes to ten one-hour daily lessons (short-term studies). When the instructional period is short we can specify the criterion measures, control the instructional content by providing the materials, give the teacher some examples of the criterion measures so that he can focus the instruction upon relevant material, observe the entire instructional period, and record it on audiotape or videotape. Studies employing this design offer the promise of focusing upon specific aspects of the teacher's role, such as the ability to explain new material, and investigators will not have to contend with other "noise," such as the teacher's managerial and disciplinary function.

Such a concern for specificity and control has led to a number of studies (e.g., Flanders, 1965; Furst, 1967; Gage *et al.*, 1968; Rosenshine, 1968a; Wright and Nuthall, 1970), and the results of these studies are included in the preceding review. Surprisingly, these studies have not yielded a larger number of significant results than have the long-term studies, nor was there any different pattern of findings. The lack of stronger results in the short-term studies has led to two suggestions. One is to determine the relevance of the classroom instruction to the criterion tests, and this will be discussed in the next section. The second suggestion is that further efforts be made to stabilize the behaviors of the teacher *before* the study is begun so that there is greater congruence between the criterion test and the teacher behaviors.

In the reported short-term studies, even though the teachers were given specific instructional materials and told the type of questions which would be on the criterion test, the use of content and cognitive processes was not controlled. As a result, in one study (Bellack *et al.*, 1966), although all teachers and their students were given the identical pamphlet, there was wide variation among classes in the content covered and in the type of cognitive processes which the teacher called for in the teacher-student interchanges. In another short-term study (Wright and Nuthall, 1970) the teachers were given outlines of the material to be covered each day and were told that the test would be factual. Yet some teachers asked open-ended questions or responded to student answers with further questions designed to raise the cognitive level of the student response. In this study the percentage of open-ended and reciprocal questions was negatively (though not significantly) related to achievement. The authors concluded that although the teachers may have been attempting to teach thinking skills through such questions, such behavior was inappropriate for the criteria of this study.

In the two examples above, there were still wide variations in the behaviors of teachers even though there was a good deal of control built into the design. In the context of these studies such variation represents "noise" because the behaviors were inappropriate to the criterion measures. We do not know what correlations between teacher behavior and student achievement would have been obtained if the teachers had been trained in criterion-specific behaviors *before* they began their instruction.

Perhaps the next step in increasing control in process-product studies would be to stabilize the teacher's behavior through training so that the observed behavior would be a more accurate reflection of the teacher's intention and/or the intentions of those who prepared the instructional material. Curriculum developers and teacher educators would have to work together on this problem. Without such cooperative work we may continue to have curriculum experts developing instructional packages without clearly specifying teacher behaviors, and teacher educators training teachers in teaching skills without clearly specifying the instructional situations in which they will be used.

Methods of Analysis

OPPORTUNITY TO LEARN In the previous section in which the major results of process-product studies were summarized, the variable "student opportunity to learn the criterion material" was cited as a consistent and significant correlate of student achievement. Such a variable has not been sufficiently considered in the analysis of process-product studies; in almost all studies no measure was taken of student opportunity to learn, and consequently all classes were treated as if they had *equal* opportunity to learn. One procedure for assessing opportunity to learn is that used in the international study (Husen, 1967) in which teachers estimated the percentage of students who had had an opportunity to learn material *of the type* exemplified by each test item. Such a procedure could be applied to studies in which standardized achievement tests or special curriculum tests were used as the criteria. For example, a teacher could be shown the questions which follow a reading selection and asked whether the students in his class had had an opportunity to learn the processes necessary to answer such questions. Similar procedures could be used for most areas, such as arithmetic concepts and problem solving, map skills, or application of biological laboratory principles. When short-term studies are conducted, the transcripts or tape recordings of the class sessions could be inspected to determine whether the criterion material was indeed covered (see Rosenshine, 1968b; Shutes, 1969).

The data on opportunity to learn have been used as a covariate to further adjust the posttest scores before searching for teacher behaviors related to the adjusted posttest measure. However, in future studies the data could also be used as a correlate of achievement, as a relevant teacher behavior contributing to student achievement.

TYPE OF STATISTICAL ANALYSIS Most investigators have used correlational statistics to determine the relationship between teacher behavior and student achievement. In such situations, both variables are treated as interval data. Other investigators have *grouped* teachers according to whether they were high, middle, or low on one of the two variables, and then used analysis of variance to test their hypotheses. In two studies in which both types of analyses were applied to the same data (Furst, 1967; Nuthall, personal communication), statistically significant results were obtained when analysis of variance was used, but *not* when correlations were computed. In the study by Furst, the scatter-plot (and the *F*-ratio) showed that the highest achieving teachers were clearly more indirect than the other teachers, although the correlation between indirectness and achievement was only .29.

If a major purpose of process-product studies is to identify variables which are promising for use in future experimental studies, it does not seem appropriate for investigators to limit themselves to any given level of statistical significance or to any one set of statistical procedures. Rather, a variety of procedures should be used to identify promising variables.

GENERIC SKILLS OF TEACHING Despite the acceptance of individual differences in education, process-product studies have still been designed as if there were one set of effective behaviors that could be applied to all students. One alternative approach is to use analysis of variance in which teachers are classified as high, middle, and low on a number of behaviors, and the class mean achievement scores are used as the cell entries. Another analytic procedure, proposed by Gage and Shutes (personal communication), is to develop a scoring scheme for a hierarchy of teacher behaviors. For example, a hierarchy might be developed in which the relevance of the instruction to the criterion test is considered first, then the cognitive level of the interaction, and then the level of affective interactions. In such a situation high positive affective behaviors by the teacher might not influence student cognitive growth if the first two conditions were not met, and therefore the scoring scheme would give less weight to teacher affective behaviors.

Almost all the process-product studies have focused upon the relationship of teacher behavior to the *class mean*. Few investigators have focused on the "personality" or "learning style" of subgroups of learners, or have stratified classes according to the initial knowledge or aptitude of the students. (For a discussion of analyses of main effects and interaction effects, see Walberg, 1970b. For an example of the study of subgroups within a class see Anderson, 1970.)

There is also the possibility that certain teaching behaviors have differential effectiveness for different types of materials and for students of different age levels. Unfortunately, there are not enough studies of any subject area even to begin to suggest different patterns of effectiveness for different materials and grade levels. Finally, we must remain aware of the possibility that teaching and learning are so idiosyncratic that we shall never find anything approaching a set or sets of effective procedures.

Summary

In the section above we have suggested modifications in the design of process-product studies and the selection and use of variables which might be useful for consideration in future studies of this type. Each of the suggestions is meant to make up for deficiencies in the current studies. Hopefully, the process-product studies which employ improved design and methodology will yield stronger results than those obtained heretofore.

Future Experimental Studies

Although hypotheses derived from the varied sources suggested above are extremely useful in teacher education programs, experimental studies provide the strongest procedures for validating the usefulness of these hypotheses.

Ideally, we would prefer that research on the validation of teacher behaviors take place *before* these behaviors are disseminated in teacher education programs. But educational practice has been to innovate and to justify the innovations with unsubstantiated "logic" or "theory." Programs that include innovations based on the opinions of educational experts have received much more attention than have programs for research on teacher behaviors. For example, ten model teacher education programs have been funded, but there has been no funding on a similar scale for programs to determine what teacher behaviors *should* be taught, or whether the behaviors we are teaching have any differential effectiveness. In our judgment, it would be more rational to fund half as many teacher education programs and to spend the rest of the money for research on teaching.

It is unlikely that sufficient research will take place *before* performance criteria are implemented in preservice or in-service teacher education programs. We propose that the evaluation and research components of the teacher education programs, the regional educational laboratories engaged in program dissemination, and the research and development centers and regional laboratories engaged in teacher education be greatly strengthened to conduct research on the *validity* of the performance criteria. Currently, the evaluation proposals in the model programs focus on how effectively the programs train teachers to behave in ways which have been predetermined in the behavioral specifications. Unfortunately, there are few if any well-developed designs for evaluation in terms of the teacher's classroom behavior and the learning engendered by the teacher in public school students. It is imperative that plans to evaluate these models include not only ways to increase our knowledge of how best to train teachers to perform specific behaviors, but more importantly, ways to increase our knowledge of the relationship between these specific teacher behaviors and measures of pupil achievement.

In practice, educators and researchers in teacher education appear to be unaware of the tentativeness and limitations of the performance criteria variables. However, the large number of current training programs provides a natural opportunity for many studies on instruction. The most important studies to be undertaken are *experimental* studies.

Experimental studies in teacher education involve a number of steps. The first step is to determine whether teachers trained for specific performance criteria behave differently in their classrooms from similar teachers who do not receive the training. But it is more important to determine whether the trained teachers engender greater cognitive or affective growth in their students compared to the controls. The hypotheses derived from process-product studies and other studies on instruction can be validated *only* through experiments of this type. When such research is completed we shall have stronger information on the importance of various performance criteria, but it is also likely that many of the skills identified in the preceding review of process-product results will not be substantiated.

It is also possible to conduct correlational studies concurrently with the experimental studies. Separate correlational studies, using some of the variables and coding procedures suggested in this paper, can be conducted for the trained and the untrained samples. Such correlational studies are particularly useful because many teaching behaviors considered to be important seldom appear in the natural repertoire of teachers. For example, although Flanders (1970) stresses the importance of teacher use of a student's idea by comparing it with one expressed earlier, or by including student ideas in a summary, such behaviors seldom appear in the typical behaviors of teachers.

One way of determining whether variations in the frequencies of use of such behaviors are related to student gain would be to examine the growth engendered in students of teachers who used these behaviors more frequently. In addition, all the suggestions for improved correlational studies could be applied in this further analysis of the results of experimental studies. Such additional analyses may yield important hypotheses which could be tested in subsequent studies.

SUMMARY

In comparison with the energy and money expended on the training of teachers, on the development and promotion of educational innovations, on the development of instructional materials, and on the work in laboratory studies of human learning, there have been few well-designed correlational or experimental studies of classroom instruction. Reports on laboratory research on meaningful human learning and on the learning of school subjects usually conclude with a few paragraphs on "implications for teaching," but these implications are seldom implemented in a teacher training program, much less studied in a systematic fashion when teachers are the mediators of instruction. Most studies on classroom instruction have been conducted by doctoral candidates, and there have been only a few large-scale experimental or correlational studies on teacher behavior and student achievement. Because of this lack of research, we have little knowledge of the relationship between teacher behavior and student growth. Given the number of competent researchers in the American Educational Research Association, such a lack of knowledge is shameful.

Those responsible for teacher education have manifested their concern for the quality of education given our youth through the preparation of the model elementary teacher education programs. However, as of this writing no one has shown that the behaviors identified in the models have any proven relevance for the real world. To be real, teacher behaviors need to be researched so that they are known to have some relationship to student outcome measures. Until this research is done, we can have little confidence that the models are providing any more hope that either teacher training or student education will be greatly improved in the foreseeable future.

We hope that such research will be conducted in the future, and that it will be a joint effort. Those involved in the training of teachers need, and should encourage and receive, much more help from educational researchers.

REFERENCES

Allen, D. W., and J. M. Cooper, 1968. *Model Elementary Teacher Education Program.* Washington, D.C.: USOE Bureau of Research, U.S. Government Printing Office FS 5.258:58022.

Amidon, E. J., P. Amidon, and B. Rosenshine, 1969. *Skills Development in Teaching Work Manual*. Minneapolis: Association for Productive Teaching.

Anderson, G. J., 1970. "Effects of Classroom Social Climate on Individual Learning." *American Educational Research Journal*, 7:135–53.

———, and H. J. Walberg, 1968. "Classroom Climate and Group Learning." *International Journal of Educational Sciences*, 2:175–80.

Anderson, R. C., *et al.*, eds., 1969. *Current Research on Instruction*. Englewood Cliffs, N.J.: Prentice-Hall, Inc.

Anthony, B. C. M., 1967. "The Identification and Measurement of Classroom Environmental Process Variables Related to Academic Achievement." Unpublished doctoral dissertation, University of Chicago.

Beiderman, D. D., 1964. "Relationship between Teaching Style and Pupil Behavior." Unpublished doctoral dissertation, University of California at Los Angeles (University Microfilms No. 64–12, 180).

Belgard, M., B. Rosenshine, and N. L. Gage, 1968. "The Teacher's Effectiveness in Explaining: Evidence on Its Generality and Correlation with Pupils' Ratings and Attention Scores," in N. L. Gage *et al.*, *Explorations of the Teacher's Effectiveness in Explaining*. Stanford: Stanford Center for Research and Development in Teaching, Stanford University (Technical Report No. 4).

Bellack, A. A., H. M. Kleibard, R. T. Hyman, and F. L. Smith, 1966. *The Language of the Classroom*. New York: Columbia University Press.

Campbell, D. T., and J. C. Stanley, 1963. "Experimental and Quasi-experimental Designs in Research on Teaching," in *Handbook of Research on Teaching*, N. L. Gage, ed. Chicago: Rand McNally and Co., pp. 171–247.

Carline, J. L., 1969. "An Investigation of the Relationship between Various Verbal Strategies of Teaching Behavior and Achievement of Elementary School Children." Unpublished doctoral dissertation, Syracuse University.

Chall, J. S., and S. C. Feldmann, 1966. *A Study in Depth of First Grade Reading*. New York: The City College of the City University of New York (U.S. Office of Education Cooperative Research Project No. 2728).

Conners, C. K., and L. Eisenberg, 1966. *The Effect of Teacher Behavior on Verbal Intelligence in Operation Headstart Children*. Baltimore: Johns Hopkins University School of Medicine (U.S. Office of Economic Opportunity Headstart Contract No. 510).

Cook, R. E., 1967. "The Effect of Teacher Methodology upon Certain Achievements of Students in Secondary School Biology." Unpublished doctoral dissertation, University of Iowa, Iowa City.

Crossman, D., and D. R. Olson, 1969. *Encoding Ability in Teacher-Student Communication Games*. Paper presented to the American Educational Research Association, February 1969. Toronto: Ontario Institute for Studies in Education.

Fey, J., 1969. "Classroom Teaching of Mathematics." *Review of Educational Research*, 39:535–51.

Flanders, N. A., 1965. *Teacher Influence, Pupil Attitudes, and Achievement.*

U.S. Office of Education Cooperative Research Monograph No. 12, OE-25040. Washington, D.C.: U.S. Government Printing Office.

———, 1970. *Analyzing Teaching Behavior.* New York: Addison-Wesley Co.

Fortune, J. C., 1966. *The Generality of Presenting Behaviors in Teaching Preschool Children.* Memphis, Tenn.: Memphis State University.

———, 1967. *A Study of the Generality of Presenting Behaviors in Teaching.* Memphis, Tenn.: Memphis State University (U.S. Office of Education Project No. 6–8468).

———, N. L. Gage, and R. E. Shutes, 1966. *The Generality of the Ability to Explain.* Paper presented to the American Educational Research Association, February 1966. Amherst: University of Massachusetts, College of Education.

Furst, N. F., 1967. *The Multiple Languages of the Classroom.* Paper presented at the meeting of the American Educational Research Association, February 1967. Also available as an unpublished doctoral dissertation, Temple University, Philadelphia, 1967.

———, and E. Amidon, 1967. "Teacher-Pupil Interaction Patterns in the Elementary School," in E. Amidon and H. Hough, eds. *Interaction Analysis: Theory, Research and Application.* Reading, Mass.: Addison-Wesley.

Gage, N. L., 1969. "Teaching Methods." *Encyclopedia of Educational Research,* 4th ed. (edited by Robert L. Ebel). A Project of the American Educational Research Association. London: The Macmillan Co., pp. 1446–58.

——— *et al.,* 1968. *Explorations of the Teacher's Effectiveness in Explaining.* Technical Report No. 4. Stanford: Stanford Center for Research and Development in Teaching, Stanford University.

Gallagher, J. J., 1968. *Analyses of Teacher Classroom Strategies Associated with Student Cognitive and Affective Performance.* U.S. Department of Health, Education, and Welfare, Office of Education, Project No. 3325, Contract No. OE-6-19-196. Urbana: University of Illinois.

———, 1970. "Three Studies of the Classroom," Chapter 4 in AERA Monograph No. 6, *Classroom Observation.* Chicago: Rand McNally and Co.

———, and M. J. Aschner, 1963. "A Preliminary Report on Analysis of Classroom Interaction." *Merrill-Palmer Quarterly,* 9:183–195.

Gunnison, J. P., 1968. "An Experiment to Determine the Effects of Changing Teacher Classroom Behavior through Training of Student-Teachers in the Use of the Flanders Interaction Analysis System." Unpublished doctoral dissertation, Arizona State University, Tempe, Arizona.

Harris, A. J., *et al.,* 1968. *A Continuation of the CRAFT Project: Comparing Reading Approaches with Disadvantaged Urban Negro Children in Primary Grades.* U.S. Office of Education Project No. 5-0570-2-12-1. New York: Division of Teacher Education of the City University of New York.

Harris, A. J., and B. Serwer, 1960. *Comparison of Reading Approaches in First Grade Teaching with Disadvantaged Children (The CRAFT Project).* U.S. Office of Education Cooperative Research Project No. 2677. New York: City University of New York.

Herman, W. L., Jr., J. E. Potterfield, C. M. Dayton, and K. G. Amershek, 1969. "The Relationship of Teacher-Centered Activities and Pupil-Centered Activities to Pupil Achievement and Interest in 18 First-Grade Social Studies Classes." *American Educaitonal Research Journal,* 6:227–40.

Hiller, J. H., G. A. Fisher, and W. Kaess, 1969. "A Computer Investigation of Verbal Characteristics of Effective Classroom Learning." *American Educational Research Journal,* 6:661–77.

Hough, J., 1968. *Specifications for a Comprehensive Undergraduate and Inservice Teacher Education Program for Elementary Teachers.* Washington, D.C.: USOE Bureau of Research, U.S. Government Printing Office, PS5.258:58016.

Houston, W. R., 1968. *Behavioral Science Elementary Teacher Education Program.* Washington, D.C.: USOE Bureau of Research, U.S. Government Printing Office, FS5.258.58024.

Hughes, M., 1962. "What Is Teaching? One Viewpoint." *Educational Leadership,* 19:251–59.

Hunter, C. P., 1969. "Classroom Climate and Pupil Characteristics in Special Classes for the Educationally Handicapped." Unpublished doctoral dissertation, University of Southern California, Los Angeles.

Husen, T., ed., 1967. *International Study of Achievement in Mathematics: A Comparison of Twelve Countries,* Vol. 2. New York: John Wiley and Sons, Inc.

Jackson, P., 1968. *Life in Classrooms.* New York: Holt, Rinehart, and Winston, Inc.

Joyce, B. R., 1968. *A Teacher Innovator: A Program to Prepare Teachers.* Washington, D.C.: USOE Bureau of Research, U.S. Government Printing Office, FS5.258:58021.

Katz, L. G., 1969. *Teaching in Preschools: Roles and Goals.* Document No. 70706-E-AO-U-26. Urbana: National Laboratory on Early Childhood Education, University of Illinois.

Kleinman, G., 1964. "General Science Teacher's Questions, Pupil and Teacher Behaviors, and Pupils' Understanding of Science." Unpublished doctoral dissertation, University of Virginia, Charlottesville, Virginia (University Microfilms No. 65–3961).

LaShier, W. S., Jr., 1967. "The Use of Interaction Analysis in BSCS Laboratory Block Classrooms," *Journal of Teacher Education,* 18:439–46.

Lea, H. M. H., 1964. "A Study of Some Characteristics of the Variability of Teacher Activities in the Social Studies and Pupil Response and Achievement." Unpublished doctoral dissertation, University of Minnesota, Minneapolis (University Microfilms No. 64–9494).

Mastin, V. E., 1963. "Teacher Enthusiasm." *Journal of Educational Research,* 56:385–86.

Medley, D. M., and H. E. Mitzel, 1959. "Some Behavioral Correlates of Teacher Effectiveness." *Journal of Educational Psychology,* 50:239–46.

Miller, G. L., 1966. "Collaborative Teaching and Pupil Thinking." *Journal of Teacher Education,* 17:337–58.

Mitzel, H. E., 1960. "Teacher Effectiveness," in Chester W. Harris, ed., *Encyclopedia of Educational Research,* 3rd ed. New York: The Macmillan Co., pp. 1481–86.

Morsh, J. E., 1956. *Systematic Observation of Instructor Behavior.* Development Report No. AFPTRC-TN-56-52. San Antonio: Air Force Personnel and Training Research Center, Lackland Air Force Base.

Nikoloff, S. E. B., 1965. "The Relationship of Teacher Standards to the Written Expression of Fifth and Sixth Grade Children." Unpublished doctoral dissertation, State University of New York at Buffalo, Buffalo, New York (University Microfilms No. 66–3520).

Nuthall, G. A., 1968. "An Experimental Comparison of Alternative Strategies for Teaching Concepts." *American Educational Research Journal,* 5:561–84.

Penny, R. E., 1969. "Presenting Behaviors and Teacher Success." Unpublished doctoral dissertation, Stanford University, Stanford.

Perkins, H. V., 1964. "A Procedure for Assessing the Classroom Behavior of Students and Teachers." *American Educational Research Journal,* 1:240–60.

———, 1965. "Classroom Behavior and Under-Achievement." *American Educational Research Journal,* 2:1–12.

Popham, W. J., 1969. "Curriculum Materials." *Review of Educational Research,* 39:319–39.

Rogers, V. M., and O. L. Davis, 1970. "Varying the Cognitive Level of Classroom Questions: An Analysis of Student Teachers' Questions and Pupil Achievement in Elementary Social Studies." Paper presented to the American Educational Research Association, March, 1970. Lexington: University of Kentucky.

Rosenshine, B., 1968a. "To Explain: A Review of Research." *Educational Leadership,* 26:303–9.

———, 1968b. "Objectively Measured Behavioral Predictors of Effectiveness in Explaining." Stanford, Calif.: Technical Report No. 4, Stanford Research and Development Center in Teaching.

———, 1970a. "Teaching Behaviors and Student Achievement." Stockholm, Sweden: International Association for the Evaluation of Educational Achievement, 1970 (mimeo).

———, 1970b. *Interpretative Study of Teacher Behaviors Related to Student Achievement.* USOE Project No. 9B–010. Philadelphia: Temple University.

———, 1970c. "Evaluation of Instruction." *Review of Educational Research,* 40:279–301.

———, 1970d. "Enthusiastic Teaching: A Research Review." *The School Review,* 78:499–515.

Ryans, D. G., 1960. *Characteristics of Teachers.* Washington, D.C.: American Council on Education.

Samph, T., 1969. "Observer Effects on Teacher Behavior." Paper delivered at the annual meeting of the American Educational Research Association, Los Angeles.

Schalock, H. D., 1968. *A Competency Based, Field Centered, Systems Approach to Elementary Teacher Education.* Washington, D.C.: USOE Bureau of Research, U.S. Government Printing Office, FS5.258:58020.

Shutes, R. E., 1969. "Verbal Behaviors and Instructional Effectiveness." Unpublished doctoral dissertation, Stanford University.

Smith, B. O., *et al.*, 1962, *A Study of the Logic of Teaching.* Urbana: University of Illinois.

Smith, B. O., M. Meux, *et al.*, 1966. *A Study of the Strategies of Teaching.* Urbana: Bureau of Educational Research, College of Education, University of Illinois.

Snider, R. M., 1966. *A Project to Study the Nature of Effective Physics Teaching.* Ithaca, New York: Cornell University (U.S. Office of Education Research Project No. S-280). Also available as an unpublished doctoral dissertation, Cornell University, 1966.

Soar, R. S., 1966. *An Integrative Approach to Classroom Learning.* Philadelphia, Pa.: Temple University (Final Report, Public Health Service Grant No. 5-R11-MH 01096 and National Institute of Mental Health Grant No. 7-R11-MH 02045). (ERIC ED: 033–479).

Solomon, D., W. E. Bezdek, and L. Rosenberg, 1963. *Teaching Styles and Learning.* Chicago: Center for the Study of Liberal Education for Adults. (ERIC ED: 026–556).

Spaulding, R. L., 1965. *Achievement, Creativity, and Self-Concept Correlates of Teacher-Pupil Transactions in Elementary Schools.* Hempstead, New York: Hofstra University (U.S. Office of Education Cooperative Research Project No. 1352).

Thompson, G. R., and N. C. Bowers, 1968. *Fourth Grade Achievement as Related to Creativity, Intelligence, and Teaching Style.* Paper presented to the American Educational Research Association, Chicago, February 1968.

Torrance, E. P., and E. Parent, 1966. *Characteristics of Mathematics Teachers that Affect Students' Learning.* U.S. Office of Educational Cooperative Research Project No. 1020, Contract No. SAE-8993. Minneapolis: Minnesota School Mathematics and Science Center, Institute of Technology, University of Minnesota.

Travers, R. M. W., 1969. "Educational Psychology." In R. L. Ebel (Ed.), *Encyclopedia of Educational Research* (Fourth Edition). London: The Macmillan Company, pp. 413–19.

Vere DeVault, M., 1969. *Wisconsin Elementary Teacher Education Project.* Madison: School of Education, University of Wisconsin.

Vorreyer, D. F., 1965. "An Analysis of Teacher Classroom Behavior and Role." Unpublished doctoral dissertation, University of Maryland, College Park.

Walberg, H. J., 1969. "Predicting Class Learning." *American Educational Research Journal,* 6:529–43.

———, 1970a. "Curriculum Evaluation: Problems and Guidelines." *Teachers' College Record,* 71:557–71.

———, 1970b. "A Model for Research on Instruction." *School Review,* 78:185–200.

———, and C. J. Anderson, 1968. "Classroom Climate and Individual Learning." *Journal of Educational Psychology,* 59:414–19.

Wallen, N. E., 1966. *Relationships between Teacher Characteristics and Student Behavior: Part Three.* U.S. Office of Education Cooperative Research Project No. SAE OE 5-10-181. Salt Lake City: University of Utah.

Welch, W. W., 1969. "Curriculum Evaluation." *Review of Educational Research,* 39:429–45.

Wittrock, M., 1962. "Set Applied to Student Teaching." *Journal of Educational Psychology,* 53:175–80.

Worthen, B. R., 1968a. "A Study of Discovery and Expository Presentation: Implications for Teaching." *Journal of Teacher Education,* 19:223–42.

———, 1968b. *Discovery and Expository Task Presentation in Elementary Mathematics.* Journal of Educational Psychology Monograph Supplement, Vol. 59, No. 1, Part 2. Washington, D.C.: American Psychological Association.

Wright, C. J., and G. Nuthall, 1970. "The Relationships between Teacher Behavior and Pupil Achievement in Three Experimental Elementary Science Lessons." *American Educational Research Journal.* In press.

Zahorik, J. A., 1969. *Teacher Verbal Feedback and Content Development.* Paper presented to the American Educational Research Association, February 1969 (mimeo).

4

A Concept of Heuristics

FREDERICK J. McDONALD

The purpose of education is to produce intelligent behavior. Teaching, one aspect of educating, is an interaction between a teacher, a person who can induce intelligent behaving, and a learner, a person who is acquiring intelligent behavior. In this study teaching will be treated as a subcategory of instruction which is one subcategory of educating. Educating may be either self-initiated and self-controlled (as when a person reads a book of his choosing) or self-initiated but other-directed (as when a student attends a lecture of his choosing), or other-stimulated and other-directed (as when a teacher assigns a book to be read). All of these arrangements may be called instruction. Teaching is limited to those instructional interactions in which the behavior of the teacher is a necessary and sufficient condition for producing learning. The study of teaching is the study of how the teaching behavior of the teacher produces intelligent behavior in a learner.

Intelligent behavior is behavior which effectively leads to achieving a goal. The goal may be any valued human purpose such as understanding the physical structure of matter, removing pollutants from the air, improving the warmth and stability of a personal relationship, or creating an effective political entity. Effectiveness in achieving a goal may be judged by many criteria. A developed physical theory, for example, is expected to organize observations or to resolve anomalies among observations. A political system is expected to mobilize people's energies and interests to create new laws or to remove inequities in society or to create better or new forms of living. Thus "intelligent behavior" embraces many different forms of human action. Evaluating behavior as intelligent or not requires considering how a person acted in the light of what he hoped to achieve.

Within specific domains of human activity, however, there are generally accepted criteria for behaving intelligently. The rules of deductive logic govern mathematical thinking; the principles of experimental design direct the actions of scientists; even the elusive arts and letters require their practitioners to follow the prevailing aesthetic. The criteria of intelligent behavior are also culturally determined. Both what is considered a goal worth pursuing and what will be considered an acceptable way of attaining it vary from time to time and from society to society.

These comments should suggest the fruitlessness of attempting to define intelligent behavior operationally except within specific contexts. The formal relation of intelligent behavior to heuristic teaching is unchanged by the specific intelligent behavior whose acquisition is to be facilitated by heuristic teaching.

But whatever the problems in defining intelligent behavior, its most salient characteristic is that it is organized. Intelligent behavior appears in the form of systems whose parts are interconnected. The opposite of intelligent behavior is random or disorganized behavior, sequences of behavior which bear no relation to each other. A behavior system may not be effective—that is, it may not attain its goal—but at a fixed point in time the behavior is intelligent, from the viewpoint of the person acting, if it is a systematic plan to attain a goal. Either the person or an observer behaves intelligently when he recognizes that the actions planned cannot or are not achieving the goal.

Intelligent behavior has five characteristics. First, it is developmental in character within species and evolutionary across species. Practically no intelligent behavior can be found in neonates except in those few and limited systems which are innate. Intelligent behavior is largely acquired by learning. Initially, intelligent behavior consists in organizing sensory events into simple, adaptive systems. Then more complex perceptual systems and rudimentary symbolic systems are acquired. Finally, complex, abstract symbolic systems are acquired which control a highly diverse response repertoire.

Second, these systems become increasingly more complex at each level of development. A language system which orders abstractions of easily perceived and coded objects develops into hierarchical coding systems of events increasingly distant. Studies of perceptual-cognitive and motor learning all show progression from acquisition of simple systems to acquisition of complex systems.

Third, these systems are information-processing systems. They are structures[1] for encoding and transforming information, for storing it, and for

[1] "Structures" are organizations of physical events. The structure of an information-processing system must be described in terms of physical events. This description includes a statement of the components and the actions to be taken on these components. An example is a computer program, which describes the method of processing specified data.

generating interactions with environmental events. These structures are relatively stable characteristics of the learner. In the past such systems have been conceptualized in many different ways; for example, as associations or stimulus-response pairs, as habit hierarchies, as cognitive maps, and as cell assemblies. Each of these earlier models, like cognitive maps and cell assemblies, comes closer to the concept of an information-processing system. But they either lack abstractness, as in stimulus-response models, thus tying the model to behavior whose topology can be mapped into the stimulus-response format, or they carry surplus meaning, as in cognitive models, or they are limited by attempting to link neurophysiological functioning and behavior.

Conceptualizing intelligent behavior as the functioning of information-processing systems generates a model whose concepts have great generality—that is, they can be used to describe and to analyze many different kinds of behavior; whose concepts are relatively few in number, and, most importantly, whose concepts can be generated in physical systems (computers).

Fourth, these systems are modified by interaction with the environment through the use of feedback mechanisms. If these modifications are permanent, we say that "learning" has occurred.

Fifth, these systems function in a steady-state system until a disturbance in the form of new input enters the system. (Again, in the past, this condition has been described as an equilibrium state, or rigidity or inflexibility, or as inhibition mechanisms. The concept used here is again more abstract and more amenable to physical construction and representation in computer systems.) Whether or not the system modifies itself to use the new input is a function of its characteristics. (Some systems are not modifiable; mentally retarded children are a relevant example.)

The above description of intelligent behavior is useful in focusing our attention on the purpose of instruction and teaching. It is to generate these systems. Before proceeding to a description of a model of instructional and teaching processes, it will be useful to describe the student as an information-processing system.

AN INFORMATION-PROCESSING MODEL OF THE LEARNER

The information-processing model of a learner has relatively few components. This simplicity results from two facts; first, the model is specifically designed to generate a described output. Second, we have at present only very general ideas about the nature of the processes which generate output from these systems. Consequently, the processes are developed mostly by tinkering.

An example will make these points more concrete. Assume that a student is to learn how to calculate the area of a circle. He must have the real number system and the meaning of the symbols A, Π, r, and $=$ encoded as a subsystem. He must be able to substitute real numbers for these symbols and to perform the specified operations on them.

In this model of an information-processing system, we need to specify those internal states of the system described above—for example, the operation of multiplying. The system must have this routine and one for substituting numbers repetitively available in it. A routine for decoding directions and one for encoding outputs completes the system.

In general, information-processing systems will have decoding and encoding systems, transformation systems, memory systems, and processes for moving data between these systems.

The physical analogue of this system has the characteristics of a finite-state machine (Minsky, 1967); hence, the model of the finite-state machine can be used to analyze the behavior of a person computing the area of a circle. The advantage of being able to describe the information-processing system as a finite-state machine is that the system can then be analyzed by generalizing the properties of a finite-state system to it. For example, we know that the system's output at any specified point in time is solely a function of its immediate history and the input in the immediately preceding time unit.

Knowing this characteristic is heuristic for generating an instructional system which will produce the information-processing system. A linear programming model controls the immediate history and simplifies it—that is, eliminates noise in the input signal. It is a heuristic choice as the instructional model.

The instructional process by which this information-processing system is produced is quite simple. We store numbers and multiplication routines in the learner. We store a substitution routine by which he places numbers in the equation defining the area of a circle. (Note: once this latter routine has been built into the system, an infinite number of calculations by formula can be made by the system.)

Significant aspects of understanding have been deliberately omitted in this example. The point of the example is to show that if the output of the system can be described, the characteristics of the information-processing system can also be described. These will be general systems such as encoding systems whose specific characteristics will have to be specified for each type of output desired.

HEURISTIC TEACHING

Obviously, learning is frequently more complex than the process described in the foregoing example. Consider, in contrast, the following example. Assume that students are given the problem of *discovering* the relation between the radius of a circle and its area. The learner must be able: (1) to identify and symbolize the radius; (2) to identify and symbolize the area; (3) to enumerate both; (4) to vary both; (5) to order the variations; (6) to detect the need for a constant multiplier. All of these systems require that the learner has stored and can retrieve data; for example, he must have stored the symbols of the real number system as well as the subroutine for multiplying real numbers.

The information-processing systems required remain the same—decoding, transformation, memory and retrieval, and encoding systems. These systems are necessary to discriminate and to categorize the input, to translate it, to recall related data, and to symbolize the output. The operations required for computing the area of a circle are *presumably* necessary for discovering the relation between the area of a circle and its radius.

We say "presumably" because we did not know what operations are necessary to discover the relationship. Any teacher who has taught inductively will recall that he has shaped the conditions, he thought, for discovering a relation, only to find that his students did not perceive it. He might, for example, construct a table listing the correlated values of r and A. The student must discover that the ratio of the area to the radius is a constant. How does he do this? He must also discover that the area is a function of the radius squared. To discover the relationship, he must generate three operations: (1) putting the successive pairs in the form A/r; (2) squaring r and forming the ratio A/r^2; (3) generating products of r^2 and the constant multiplier to test the relation.

The concept of heuristics and of heuristic teaching are evident in these three operations. First, no logical way of deriving these relations is apparent in the problem as initially presented. Second, there seems to be a certain "chancy" character to hitting upon relations—if one is clever enough to manipulate the relations between two sets of numbers, he will discover that the ratio A/r is a constant.

These manipulations are *heuristics*. "Heuristic" derives from the Greek verb, "to discover" (*heuriskein*). "Heuristic" as an adjective, as in "heuristic teaching," means "serving to guide, discover, or reveal." A heuristic is tentative and intuitive in character—"valuable for empirical research but unproved or incapable of proof." Heuristic thinking is a way of thinking that leads to the solution of a problem. Its value derives from its demonstrated utility in solving problems or making a discovery. In mathematics, for example, seeing analogies between a problem that has been solved and one that is being solved generates insight into a solution. A common heuristic familiar to students of plane geometry is the use of auxiliary lines to redesign a figure. The new figure suggests relationships which can be elucidated and developed into a systematic proof of a theorem.

There is no logic or theory that says if you play with numbers by multiplying them or dividing them or adding them or subtracting them, you will discover a relation between two concepts enumerated by these numbers. But such manipulations frequently work—that is, they do produce a discovery.

Perhaps there is a kind of commonsense logic something like this: "If somebody says, 'What is the relation between the radius of a circle and its area?' there must be one; given these sets of numbers, I know that there are four basic operations I can perform on them, so why not try them?"

Obviously, the learner must find some way of organizing the data or of reconceptualizing the problem so that he "sees" the functional relation between these variables.

The Infinite-State Model

The finite state model of an information-processing system obviously does not describe the behavior required to discover a relation. There is no linear, orderly way of performing operations to discover a relation. The finite memories of such systems are too limited for discovering relations.

The metaphor that describes the differences between finite-state and infinite-state models is that the infinite-state model is a finite-state model with unlimited "scratch paper." An infinite-state model is a system which has an infinite memory and can recursively explore it.

A infinite-state information-processing system is an instruction-obeying system. But the controlling process which guides the operations of the machine is what is called an "effective procedure." "An effective procedure is a set of rules which tell us, from moment to moment, precisely how to behave" (Minsky, 1967, p. 106). The system which operates on an effective procedure must have a *language* in which sets of behavioral rules are to be expressed and a system which interprets statements in the language.

The key concept is this description of the infinite-state model is the concept of an effective procedure. An effective procedure is a set of rules, but the infinite-state model, unlike the finite-state model which also operates under rules, generates successive states which are interdependent in the sense that the rule to be followed at step two is a function of the output of step one, and may be one of an infinite number of rules that might be tried. The system selects the guiding rule at each step as a function of where it arrived in the preceding step, but the selection is from an infinite pool of possibilities.

The system requires two features, a "search" capacity, and "gimmicks," the latter being rules and procedures whose logic is unknown. Both systems constitute sets of heuristics for problem-solving. The first system is a set of heuristics for search, the second, a set of heuristics for testing solutions or presolutions to problems.

The advantage of conceptualizing problem-solving or "discovery" in terms of this model is that the characteristics of these models are known (Minsky,

1967) and can be generalized to information-processing systems in the same way that we suggested the characteristics of finite-state models could be generalized. The generalization process will also suggest heuristic models of instructional processes.

Effective Procedures as Heuristics

An effective procedure is a heuristic in the sense that when used it works—that is, it produces a desired result. Search procedures similarly may be thought of as effective procedures or heuristics since they are rules for selecting among the first set of effective procedures or heuristics.

An information-processing system such as a learner must acquire both kinds of effective procedures if he is to solve problems. Otherwise, he must act as a finite system carrying out preprogrammed routines.

Heuristic Teaching as Effective Procedures

The task of instructing and teaching may be conceptualized as defining those conditions under which the learner as an information-processing system may be most conveniently conceptualized as a finite-state model or as an infinite-state model. Once this decision is made, the task is either to program him using the linear programming model as the instructional model or to teach him effective procedures or heuristics using heuristic teaching as the instructional model.

Heuristic teaching is an infinite-state information-processing model designed to produce effective procedures or heuristics in a learner so that he may solve problems or acquire intelligent behavior. The only existing "machine" with this potentiality is a human being. The problem is to train or educate him so that he functions as this kind of a system.

THE LEARNING OF HEURISTICS

The basic problem in developing heuristic teaching is twofold: (1) to learn what heuristics are relevant to particular domains of problems; (2) to devise the instructional strategies which are heuristic in inducing problem-solving. The first problem is complicated by the fact that heuristics emerge inductively within a discipline but may be generalized across disciplines. For example, one heuristic very useful in solving problems in mathematics and the physical sciences is to reduce the problem to the simplest case. Its general applicability is seen in the fact that it also has utility in scene design in the theater, in painting, and in writing.

There is no science of heuristics, though one may develop. As method, heuristics has received some but relatively little attention in contrast to the study of methods of logical proof, the principles of measurement, experimental design, and the philosophy of theory-building and hypothesis-testing. Polya states the method to be used in understanding and developing heuristic: "Experience in solving problems and experience in watching other people solving problems must be the basis on which heuristic is built" (Polya, 1957, p. 130). The analytic method may be one of the following: (1) the reconstruction of problem-solving by individuals by examining their writings and other descriptions of how they worked; (2) the analysis of observed problem-solving behavior; (3) the development of simulations of mental operations. The work of historian-scientists is an example of the first method (Kuhn, 1962); the classical studies of problem-solving (Duncker, 1945; Wertheimer, 1959) and the work of Piaget illustrates the second method; and the work on artificial intelligence and computer simulation of verbal learning (Feigenbaum and Feldman, 1963) illustrates the third.

There has been some attempt to codify the heuristics in mathematics (Polya, 1957). Also, Wertheimer's work (1959) may be seen as a study of heuristics and particularly the heuristics of search. Most of the ideas in that book may be translated into the concepts of information-processing models. Another source of ideas on heuristics is emerging out of the study of heuristic programming in computer science (Feigenbaum and Feldman, 1963).

Studies of discovery learning (Shulman and Keisler, 1966) are interesting to analyze in terms of the concepts used in this paper. A learner in an experimental condition in which he receives no prompts may or may not be an infinite-state information processing system. This condition can be effective for learning only if the persons in it can function as such systems. If they lack either effective procedures (as used previously) or heuristics, they cannot solve problems. If the problem is to discover a relation, the learner must have the heuristics available to discover the relation. If he does not, he cannot discover it.

There is no reason to believe that searching will produce learning; obviously, the search may be ineffective. The theory of infinite-state models suggests that learning of effective procedures can occur, but such learning presupposes that a minimum set of effective procedures is present in the system. Discovering the conditions under which such learning occurs is an exceedingly complex problem, one not likely to be quickly solved. The first step should be finding effective procedures and discovering heuristics for locating and using them. The second step is to discover heuristic teaching strategies.

The literature of discovery learning should be reexamined to find out what kinds of heuristic teaching strategies were implicitly built into them. These strategies, which inevitably will involve some form of prompting or eliciting, can be used as a starting point for conceptualizing heuristic teaching strategies. They will also involve ways of setting problems, ways of inducing and breaking sets, and ways of prompting reformulation or transformations of problems.

So little is known that one can begin anywhere and make progress. But what must be avoided is the misconceptualizations of the past—that discovery learning should be contrasted with rote learning, or inductive teaching with deductive teaching. The problem is, given a problem to solve, how are effective procedures or heuristics built into the information systems of the learner so that he can solve the problem, and how are the strategies for building in these heuristics and for eliciting them learned by a teacher. That is what the study of heuristic teaching is all about.

REFERENCES

Duncker, K., 1945. "On Problem Solving." *Psychological Monographs,* No. 270.

Feigenbaum, E., and J. Feldman, 1963. *Computers and Thought.* New York: McGraw-Hill Book Company.

Kuhn, Thomas S., 1962. *The Structure of Scientific Revolutions.* Chicago: University of Chicago Press.

Minsky, M., 1967. *Computation: Finite and Infinite Machines.* Englewood Cliffs, N.J.: Prentice-Hall, Inc.

Polya, G., 1957. *How to Solve It,* 2nd ed. Garden City, N.Y.: Doubleday and Company, Inc.

Shulman, L., and E. Keisler, eds., 1966. *Learning by Discovery: A Critical Appraisal.* Chicago: Rand McNally and Co.

Wertheimer, M., 1959. *Productive Thinking.* New York: Harper and Row, Publishers.

5

Promoting Self-Disciplined Learning: A Researchable Revolution

ROBERT F. PECK

PRESENT EDUCATION: AN OTHER-DIRECTED SYSTEM OF MASS PRODUCTION

"Discipline" is usually talked about as a matter of controlling groups of students. Ostensibly, the aim is to minimize interference with student learning. Often, though, an honest look would make it clear that an overriding aim is to minimize student behavior that disturbs the adults on the scene. In any case, most discussions of discipline talk about generalized tactics which generalized teachers can use to control generalized masses of students. There is a certain charm of economy in this approach. If one or two methods would bring about "good discipline," that would make the job a lot easier. In a constructive way, Kounin's (1970) research appears to identify just such generalized strategies which show positive effects on children's attention to the business of learning. Closer examination of such teacher skills as "with-it-ness," to be sure, suggest that the teacher had better be alert to differential behavior by different students so that he can rapidly make complex judgments about which student to address and the appropriate way to deal with that specific child's actions. Nonetheless, the logic of the approach is to seek a few generalizable procedures for "disciplining" large groups of students.

But what is "good discipline," really? Another honored tradition in American education identifies the desirable end product as people who are self-directing, divergent-thinking (Torrance, 1965), self-actualizing (Maslow, 1954)—in short, *self*-disciplining individuals. We say this. Do we believe it or do we practice it?

There is a great deal of evidence for the proposition that we do not practice it. Flanders (1969) summarized much research by saying that teachers "talk between 65 and 75 percent of the time . . . ," and in such fashion, moreover, that what "pupils' verbal communication occurs is primarily in response to the initiative of the teacher." Gallagher (1965) observed that most pupils respond in terms of pure memory to rather rigid patterns of teacher stimulation. Flanders concluded,

> The preponderance of evidence . . . would indicate that most . . . teachers could adopt patterns which are more responsive to the ideas and opinions expressed by pupils and realize a gain in both positive pupil attitudes and pupil achievement [p. 1429].

It might be added that such teaching would at least *allow* for children to exercise more self-initiated behavior. Given suitable intermittent guidance by the teacher, they might learn to discipline themselves rather than be always controlled by the ever-present teacher.

In another recent study, Susskind (1969) noted,

> . . . in this not atypical school, the children do not ask questions, while the teachers ask an incredibly large number of questions. Further, the teachers and administrators are strongly opposed to this situation in theory, but are unaware that it exists in their classrooms.

He goes on to say that this is not because students don't talk at all, but because less than a tenth of all they say is question-asking.

> We suspect that the negative correlation [between teacher questioning and student questioning] is due to a particular pattern of teacher question-asking, a pattern that students do not find intellectually stimulating and gratifying. This pattern . . . involves a high rate of TQ [teacher questioning] that permits no time for discussion or reflection, in which the questions are predominantly factual, right or wrong, convergent questions, relying on memory and the parroting back of the text.

Medley (1970) quotes Phillip Jackson's observation that even in a

> very progressive, modern nursery school . . . he found that the kids were actually free to initiate and carry through an action only five percent of the time; ninety-five percent of the youngsters' actions were essentially dictated. Now that is astounding. . . . I don't think a teacher could believe she was doing this.

In short, contemporary practice seems largely to treat students as passive, teacher-controlled units in an almost faceless mob. Certainly, the tiny proportion of time in which any one student can openly express thoughts or feelings of his own stringently restricts any teacher's chances of truly getting to know that student. The evidence indicates, moreover, that there is extremely little provision in our schools for the development of *individual initiative* in any way that could lead to wisely self-disciplined action, when the chance for independent action ultimately does arise.

Our mass production system is even inefficient by its own measures of productivity. The middle-class students who least need schooling, considering the high level of infectious literacy they experience at home, do graduate from high school, even from college. On the other hand, more than fifty percent of the students from the families of unskilled and skilled workers fail to finish high school. Throughout our history this has been the case; but we do not now retain or train these students much better than we did one hundred years ago.

Ironically, the massive inertia of these educational habits even shapes the ideas and the tools of the most progressive research aimed at correcting these faults. Until Spaulding (1966) and Brophy and Good (1969), systems for analyzing classroom interaction have treated the individual teacher as one actor in the educational drama. The other actor has been the-class-as-a-whole—a mechanical summation of responses of totally anonymous students, wiping out all individual differences. Such methods for interaction analysis have valuable uses but they are of *no* use for finding out what the individual student is doing, let alone how the teacher's actions are affecting him. Such systems inherently continue to divert the teacher from examining what she does to the individual student or how well it works.

The Need for Personalized, Individualized Teaching

Another irony can be found in the fact that American educators have long extolled the virtues of educating the free man in ways addressed to his unique, individual needs. There is no lack of desire or will here. A generation ago, Prescott (1945) exemplified the child study movement as an approach to truly informed diagnosis of the individual's specific abilities, needs, and readiness. Almost every undergraduate teacher-to-be in America does at least one "case study." Yet, to date, the effect on teaching practices has been so minimal as to be almost untraceable, it appears. (No research evidence could be found which either refutes or substantiates this contention.)

One does not have to look very far to perceive the reasons for this failure to carry out a sincere and good intent. Some reasons are intensely practical—for example, expense beyond what any public agency was willing to pay until recently. In addition, the goal behaviors, the assessment technology for measuring progress, and the precise instructional practices that produce self-disciplined learning have not been developed or empirically tested until now.

As Smith (1969b) says,

> It does little good for a teacher to understand that he should accept the child and build on what he is if the teacher does not know how to assess what the child brings and lacks the skills necessary to work with him. Acceptance and respect for a child as a human being, belief in his potential, and understanding of his social and emotional situation are all very good when they are expressed in appropriate teaching performances. In the abstract, they are little more than pious expressions. The experienced teacher, in search of help in his efforts to work more effectively with children, might in justice lament, "Show me not the end without the means" [p. 155].

Training Teachers to Maximize Student Coping Effectiveness

Fortunately, the current *zeitgeist* has fostered the development of most of the means for helping teachers to individualize their teaching and even to direct it toward responsible, independent thinking and action by students. The means consist of newly evolved idea systems, new methods of measurement embodying these ideas, and new techniques for educating people in a self-checking, self-correcting way. These are briefly outlined in the table. (It will be seen later that the term "effective coping" may be used to summarize the elements of healthily independent initiative, judgment, and action that are the goals of this proposed system.)

THE TOOLS FOR TRAINING TEACHERS

Conceptual System *	*Action*	*Measurement* †
Consultant behavior aimed at facilitating teacher coping	Consultant-teacher interaction	1. Coding systems for interviews 2. Consultant's observation log
Teacher coping behavior (Goals for the teacher-educator)	Teacher-child interaction	1. Videotape codes 2. Coping measures
Child coping behavior (Goals for the teacher)	Child's individual coping attitudes and actions	1. Videotape codes a. CASES b. Brophy-Good Dyadic Interaction Codes 2. Coping measures 3. Teacher observations

* The elements in these three systems should be either specifically identical, or else logically linked in a cause-effect chain, so as to permit exact statements of relational hypotheses.

† The elements in these measures should similarly be identical or logically linked so as to permit precise testing of relational hypotheses.

AN ACTION-RESEARCH MODEL

Using the tools now available, it is possible to mount experiments in teacher education which will identify more precisely than before what methods, in a given teacher's hands, will maximize the self-realizing, coping behavior of each individual student. (It should still be possible to group and instruct together students of similar needs and readiness. Such similarity is better achieved through empirical matching of students whose individual needs are alike, not merely by some simple, crude criterion such as age or IQ.)

To understand a human individual it is necessary to study that individual. Applied to teaching, this means that some part of the teacher's day must be devoted to studying one or more students individually. The case study approach is scarcely new. The work of the Bank Street College is an excellent illustration of a sophisticated use of this strategy. It has been possible to find only one study, however, which empirically tests the proposition that such knowledge about individual students makes a difference in teaching effectiveness (Sturgis, 1958). In this study, teachers of physics who were given insight into their students' personal backgrounds and characteristics produced significantly greater student gains in achievement and were rated as more effective by their students.

There is a great deal of evidence that individual differences in students make a significant difference in their response to any given method of instruction. Calvin, Hoffman, and Harden (1957) found that less intelligent students did better in group problem-solving situations conducted in an authoritarian manner than in groups conducted in a permissive manner. The same difference did not occur for bright students. Much other evidence to the same effect was summarized by McKeachie (1963). The effects of training teachers to understand individual children are almost unresearched, however, let alone the differential effects of particular teachers on particular kinds of students.

The only discoverable study ever conducted which tackled the complex interaction of different teacher types with different pupil types was done by Heil and Washburne (1962). The logic of that design is being extended in the Texas study described below.

A teacher education program aimed at personalized teaching requires a conceptual system that helps teachers accurately identify (1) the needs, abilities, and pressures that explain why a given child acts as he does; (2) goal characteristics in the child's behavior, to orient the teacher's efforts and to serve as a checklist for measuring the child's progress toward more effective learning and coping behavior; and (3) what the teacher is actually doing in her interaction with the student. Then there must be tools that embody these concepts, enabling teachers to become increasingly effective and autonomous in deciding what to do with a given student. These procedures include diagnostic assessment methods, observation records, cumulative case files, and similar materials. In addition, there are peer rating systems and observations by other staff members which can be called upon. Well-organized procedures are necessary for recording and playing back what the teacher does and how the *individual* child reacts. These may use audiotape, videotape, or observer records. Finally, the teacher needs an organizational climate that supports and facilitates such teaching.

It is not enough just to put such tools in the hands of teachers, however, without testing the actual effects. A system of ideas, tools, and data gathering procedures is also needed in order to plan a carefully specified teacher education program and to subject such a program to scientific assessment. A number of major research questions are at issue. One concerns the sources of variance in the teacher behavior which presumably results from the training program. This would include questions about the clarity and appropriateness of the ideas and tools the teacher is trained to use; the nature of the interaction process between the teacher educator and the teacher; and the willingness, ability, and interest of different teachers to respond to the training program. (There is no reason why every teacher should be forced to undertake this kind of intensively individualized and personalized interaction with students. Subject-oriented teachers can be excellent instructors, leaving the personalization to other members of a school team.)

Another research goal consists of several sets of taxonomies which do not now exist. One would identify the personal characteristics of teachers who find it natural to use Type I instructional practice, Type II practice, etc.; and the characteristics of teachers who find it notably difficult or unacceptable to use one or another type of instructional practice. A second typology would identify the aspects of student behavior that characterize significantly different modes of effective and ineffective learning. A third taxonomy would specify different instructional practices, including differences in content and method, that demonstrably produce improved learning in students of specified types.

Still further, inductive research is needed to identify the teacher education strategies that work most effectively with each kind of teacher for each kind of instructional practice.

In addition to these aspects of teacher training, it is necessary, where a teacher cannot personally "reach" certain children, to train her to search out and use, without feeling apologetic, other staff members, other curricular resources, or other instructional media which could help the teacher to diagnose and prescribe more effectively—or, indeed, which might do the instructional job and not require further action by the teacher.

The aims of such a program can be summarized in this way:

1. To discover methods of educating teachers which will enable teacher educators, supervisors and other change agents to:
2. Modify the teachers'
   a. Perceptions of children
   b. Conceptual systems for understanding children
   c. Conceptual systems for analyzing their own teaching behavior
   d. Standards for evaluating the results of their teaching (their behavioral objectives for students)
   e. Repertoire of tactics for giving differentiated, individualized instruction to different children
   f. Methods of securing and using factual feedback from pupil responses; all with the aim of:
3. Changing pupils' behavior in the direction of more effective coping, in ways appropriate to the needs and capabilities of each child.

RESEARCH STEPS IN THE PROGRAM

1. Measure the initial coping behavior, knowledge, and attitudes of each child who is to be individually instructed. This would undoubtedly be a small number of pupils for any given teacher at any one time.
2. Measure the initial coping behavior, knowledge, and attitudes of each teacher in terms relevant to the objectives of the program.
3. Record the teacher-child interaction process at intervals.
4. Record the selected pupils' behavior at the same intervals.
5. Record the interaction between the teacher educator and the teacher. This would consist of a series of sessions addressed to diagnosing the individual needs of the selected pupils, working out instructional tactics which the teacher will try, assessing the effects of the trial instruction, redesigning the instruction, and assessing the ultimate effects of the instruction on the child's coping behavior. The effects on the teacher's preference for different instructional strategies should also be assessed.
6. Assess changes in the teacher's instructional operations, pre-to-post (e.g., nine months), (a) with the selected pupils, (b) with other pupils who are both similar and different from the selected pupils, in order to ascertain the generalizing effect of the training on the teacher's instructional behavior.
7. Assess changes in the selected pupils' coping behavior, pre-to-post. Also, assess changes in the other pupils in the same classes in order to measure the effects of the teachers' tactics on both similar and different pupils.

8. Analyze the teacher-pupil interaction data to seek regularities of relationship between teacher tactics and the amount and kinds of pupil change, for combinations of different teachers and different kinds of children.
9. Analyze the consultant-teacher interaction data to seek relationships between consultant procedures and the changes in each teacher's choice of instructional strategies with different pupils. Different effects of the same kind of consultant intervention may be found with different teachers.

BACKGROUND RESEARCH

Coping Theory

Lois Murphy (1962) was the first to conduct empirical research on the coping behavior of children. She and her colleagues developed a quite detailed operational description of dimensions of coping behavior. Kroeber (1963) described coping activity, largely in intra-psychic terms. Bruner (1966) and Lazarus (1966) further discussed theoretical aspects of coping behavior, and, in the former case, reported informal observations in the school setting. Coelho *et al.* (1969) conducted a study of the characteristics of college freshmen who survived or failed to survive in their first year. Coping behavior is variously described by these various writers but, in brief, they all appear to agree that effective coping behavior includes actively confronting problems, showing independent initiative in seeking solutions, and displaying persistent effort to arrive at solutions. It is also widely held, as in Coopersmith's work (1967), that attitudes toward the problems of everyday living are an important element in coping. Similarly, attitudes toward oneself seem to be important determiners of effective coping behavior.

In a cross-national study (Peck, 1965), research personnel in eight countries, ranging from Japan to Brazil, Yugoslavia, and the United States, have independently arrived at a generally accepted definition of coping behavior. The high degree of international agreement in this study suggests that there may be a generally valid definition of effective coping, even though there are certain differences of detail in different cultures.

Adult Influences on Child Coping

Smith (1969a) observed,

> Neither the theory nor the technology of classroom management and control has been worked out. Partly as a result of the failure of psychological

> concepts to yield practical measures, research on discipline has shifted from mere theorizing about the handling of misbehavior by inferences from psychological concepts and principles to the empirical study of teacher behavior and its effects.
>
> Empirical studies have revealed new dimensions of disciplinary behavior. Such behavior may exhibit different properties from moment to moment: firm, rough, clear and so on. And the effects of these properties upon pupil behavior may vary from pupil to pupil, depending upon the pupil's maturity and his relation to the conduct toward which the control techniques are directed. Pupils may react to these qualities of teacher behavior in a number of ways [p. 295].

For example, Gibb and Gibb (1952) found that students who were actively involved in analyzing problems and deciding what to do about them "were significantly superior in role flexibility and self-insight to the students taught by traditional lecture-discussion methods." Sandefur (1967) similarly found that student teachers who were trained by means of videotaped feedback to maximize their use of indirect teaching methods made their pupils significantly more alert, responsible, confident, and self-initiating than pupils of conventionally trained teachers. Similar results have also been reported by Ojemann (1962), Pankratz (1967), Filson (1957), Flanders *et al.* (1963), and Miller (1964). Orme and Purnell (1968) found that training teachers to reinforce pupils selectively for individual compliance with pupil-set standards of classroom conduct "led to relatively stable and desirable modifications in pupil behavior."

This small number of studies is not focused, in almost any case, on the specific effects of teaching behavior on the coping behavior of individual children. There is some suggestive evidence in the literature on training for creativity. Nicholsen (1959) and Maltzman (1960) found creativity to be trainable and to be differentially influenced by different instructional tactics. Insofar as creativity may be related to independent thinking and initiative in seeking solutions to problems, this evidence may be relevant for the design of instruction aimed at producing more effective coping behavior in children.

Somewhat more distant but still related may be the findings of Coopersmith (1967) and Murphy (1962) on parental behavior associated with child coping characteristics. Murphy found that "autonomy permitted by mother" correlated significantly with such aspects of child coping behavior as sense of self-worth, resistance to discouragement, ability to mobilize energy to meet challenge or stress, differentiation of self and others, and ability to solve problems directly. Coopersmith found that the parents of children who were high in self-esteem expected them to achieve successfully, were relatively firm and decisive in dealing with them, but also felt that their children had a right to question the thinking of their parents, to express their own points of view, and to have some say in the making of family plans.

Educational Influences on Teachers

There is extremely little in the literature by way of empirical research on the effects of specified kinds of teacher education on subsequent teacher behavior. Blumberg and Amidon (1965) found that indirect supervisors, in the eyes of the teachers they worked with, were much more productive, fostered more learning, and established a more communicative atmosphere than did more directive supervisors. Blumberg (1968) subsequently found that student teacher supervisors who used indirect techniques of instruction produced appreciably more favorable effects in their student teachers.

In one of the few follow-up studies of teacher behavior after graduation, Sandefur *et al.* (1969) found that teachers who had been trained in indirect methods of instruction continued to "become significantly more responsible, more understanding, more kindly, more original, more confident, more mature and integrated" during their first year on the job. The specially trained teachers also expanded their tendencies to accept pupil feelings, to use praise and encouragement, and to accept pupil ideas.

In Davis' teaching laboratory program at the Texas Research and Development Center, it has been found that self-administered audiotape feedback during trial teaching made students evoke more pupil-initiated ideas and also made them more flexibly diversified in the range of instructional tactics they used (Davis and Smoot, 1969). Another study compared the effectiveness of trial teaching without feedback, with unguided audiotape feedback, with guided listening to tape feedback, and with nondirective supervisory feedback after listening. The supervisory consultation proved to be significantly more effective than the other training methods in getting the students to gain and increase pupil attention. Unguided, solitary listening produced no such change in teaching behavior (Morse, Kysilka, and Davis, 1969). A third study used trial teaching of fellow students, with guiding instructions, audiotape feedback, and peer feedback. This was compared with a method which presented the questioning behavior to be learned, a general group discussion, and an instructional game, but which did not include the experience of trial teaching with feedback. The active, trial teaching experience proved more effective (Morse and Davis, 1970).

In an experimental study on the effects of personalizing the education of teachers, Fuller, Peck *et al.* (1969) found that feedback from personal assessment data and feedback from videotaped teaching episodes, when conducted in a highly personalized, open-ended manner, led to significant improvements in the open-mindedness, self-confidence, and career dedication of student teachers. This treatment also increased their tendency to use more indirect teaching techniques, thereby encouraging more initiative and independence in their pupils.

In studies of microteaching, Johnston (1969) found significant changes, akin to those reported by McDonald (1968):

> [When an experiment] cued a teacher on positive instances of the desired behavior while viewing his video-taped teaching performance [it] was a highly effective training condition. . . . In this case, the teachers were being rewarded for rewarding students for participating in teacher-student dialogues. In the most effective treatment, teachers were also cued on those places where they *might* have used the desired teaching behavior. Thus, the teacher trainees were being given practice in feedback on applying a psychological concept of teaching.

By contrast with both the Texas and the Stanford methods of giving instructional feedback to teachers, Salomon and McDonald (1969) studied the effects of having student teachers watch themselves, alone, on videotape. They reported, "When no model of good teaching is presented, no guidance is given and no new and common standards are adopted, reactions to self-viewing of one's teaching performance on videotape are determined largely by the viewer's previous position." In other words, self-confrontation without external feedback leads to little change in behavior.

In summarizing the intended aims of teacher education, Clarke (1968) cited certain "general truths" about effective teaching which it is hoped teachers will learn to apply in designing their instruction for selected children within the total class setting. He cited these principles:

1. All behavior (including misbehavior) is caused.
2. Group forces profoundly influence individual behavior.
3. Learning involves mild anxiety but strong anxiety is disruptive.
4. Deflecting behavior impulses is better than prohibiting them.
5. Positive inducements (praise, success in work tasks, fulfilled needs, etc.) produce more predictable (and more desirable?) results than do negative deterrents.
6. Learning is more effective and retention is better in a warm, friendly atmosphere.

Smith (1969b) outlined the necessary elements in a sound process for educating teachers: establishment of the practice situation, specification of the behavior, performance of the specified behavior, feedback of information about the performance, modification of the performance in the light of the feedback, and a performance-feedback-correction-practice schedule which is continued until desirable skillfulness is achieved.

AN ILLUSTRATIVE STUDY

An experimental program designed along these lines is now under way in the Research and Development Center for Teacher Education in Austin,

Texas. It has been applied in elementary schools and high schools serving both advantaged children and disadvantaged, ethnic minority children. For a number of research purposes, all children and participating teachers contribute a diversified array of measures of interest, attitude, and coping style at the beginning and end of the school year. Many of these measures were developed in the cross-national study of coping styles.

Six videotapes are made of each class during the year, as well. These tapes are objectively coded for teacher behavior by the FAIR (Fuller Affective Interaction Records) and OScAR (Observation Schedule and Record Techniques) systems and another, cognitive-focused system. The tapes are coded for child coping behavior by the FAIR system, Spaulding's CASES (Coping Analysis Schedules for Educational Settings) and the Brophy-Good Dyadic Interaction system.

The crux of the method, however, is to have the teacher select a few children for intensive, year-long study and experimental instruction. All of the staff resources of the school—other teachers, the principal, the counselor, the "helping teacher," the curriculum consultants—are involved as needed. In addition, a behavioral consultant from the university part of the Research and Development complex works as a partner with the teacher. The object is to use the teacher's own observations, the assessment data, the videotapes, and anything anyone else knows to help the teacher tune in to the capacities, the motives, and the feelings of each of the children she selects for special study. In the light of such a diagnostic analysis, she then tries to tailor her treatment of the child to his specific situation. She and her consultants then observe whether her tactic works or does not work. The next stage is to discuss and revise her tactics with that child. The child is at no time aware that he is being singled out for this special attention. Most of the time in class, needless to say, the teacher is dealing with other pupils or with the class as a whole.

Obviously, no teacher could find the time to attend this intensively to every child in an elementary class of thirty or in high school groups of 150. Nonetheless, as teachers learn to focus sharply on three or four children, they report that they begin to look with new insight at many of the other children in class, in the few moments a day when they get the chance. Research is underway, of course, to measure the amount of this "radiation" effect, if it occurs.

In this program the teacher strives to select or invent learning experiences appropriate to the most urgent needs of the particular child. These experiences include selective assignments of standard instructional procedures, but they also go beyond this to include the involving of other resource people, both within and outside of the school staff, when those people may have special knowledge or skill that will aid the pupil. The teacher brings to bear al[illegible] knowledge of alternative curricular materials and strategies. With the aid of the program consultants, she learns to become more clearly and accurately aware of the child's central concerns, feelings, and motives so that her instructional planning is tailored to the real nature of that one child, not just a matter of hopeful guesswork and trial-and-error.

Since the teacher is helped to identify highly specific goals for the child, and since she participates in systematic observation of the effects of her tactics, she can diversify her tactics and become more flexibly responsive to the child's reactions in a very specific, well-aimed manner. This is quite the opposite of unguided eclecticism or vague "flexibility."

The properties of this training system that may be most potent are these:

1. It takes place in the classroom, not in some far-removed workshop or university course.
2. The child's responses follow immediately, or closely, on the teacher's actions.
3. Instant or early feedback on the child's response is available to the teacher.
4. A strenuous effort is made to trace cause and effect very closely, from consultant input to teacher action to child response.
5. The goal-behaviors for the individual child are closely specified by the teacher and her consultants; these are not limited to test performance alone, but to the growth of sound, independent judgment, initiative in tackling problems, and self-respecting, self-disciplined work at mastering problems.

A school where such a program is operating can be an excellent training ground for preservice teachers as well. Indeed, without such a live model, with room to do it oneself, it is difficult to see how a student teacher could effectively learn to perform this kind of teaching.

Research is also on foot to study exactly what kinds of consultant input lead to effective changes in teacher tactics. Tape recordings of all consultations between the consultant and the teacher are coded by a system resembling Blumberg's. In addition, each consultant maintains a detailed log of interchanges with teachers and with other members of the school staff. Research is also underway to study the effects a given teaching procedure has on different kinds of pupils, and what characteristics of teachers predispose them to use certain methods most effectively or deal with certain kinds of children best.

Needless to say, the systematic audit of the aptitude/achievement ratio, motivation, and personality patterns of all the children in a school turns up a great many problems which were previously unknown, early enough for preventive action to be taken if there is someone willing and able to take it. The help of many community agencies can be efficiently involved, as needed, when children with special needs or special problems are identified. Unlike earlier case study experiments, this design requires the specification of teaching procedures, objective assessment of how they were carried out, and measurement of their effects on child behavior. Unlike either microteaching or most forms of training in interaction analysis, this design focuses on the teacher's specific interactions with individual children, and the consequences in individual cases.

Empirical analysis of this complex web of data may not vindicate the expectation that a particular tactic in training teachers always has the desired effect of producing more self-initiated, self-disciplined behavior in the pupils. All general models for describing "good teaching" have the weakness that they ignore the children for whom the model does not work or the teacher who cannot or will not use the model. The design described here makes it possible to find out what method, in whose hands, produces teacher behavior that regularly produces positive effects on the coping behavior of a given kind of pupil. Eventually, a long way down the road, we may have a suitably complex map of the way to train different teachers effectively to individualize their instruction of children. It will take a very complex map, indeed, to match the complexities of the real world of the school. It will take lengthy, expensive, multivariate research to develop and validate such a map. At least, though, it is now possible to start.

REFERENCES

Blumberg, Arthur, 1968. "A System for Analyzing Supervisor-Teacher Interaction." Unpublished doctoral dissertation, Syracuse University.

Blumberg, Arthur, and Edmund Amidon, 1965. "Teacher Perceptions of Supervisor-Teacher Interaction." *Administrator's Notebook,* 14:1. University of Chicago Midwest Administration Center.

Brophy, J. E., and T. L. Good, 1969. "Teachers' Communication of Differential Expectations for Children's Classroom Performance." Report Series No. 25, R & D Center for Teacher Education, The University of Texas at Austin.

Bruner, Jerome S., 1966. *Toward a Theory of Instruction.* Cambridge: Harvard University Press.

Calvin, A. D., F. K. Hoffman, and E. L. Harden, 1957. "The Effect of Intelligence and Social Atmosphere on Group Problem-Solving Behavior." *Journal of Social Psychology,* 45:61–74.

Clarke, S. C. T., 1968. "Classroom Discipline." Alberta Teachers Association, Improvement of Instruction Series No. 8. Edmonton, Barnett House.

Coelho, G. V., F. Solomon, C. Wolff, A. Steinberg, and D. A. Hamburg, 1969. "Predicting Coping Behavior in College." *Journal of Nervous and Mental Disease,* 149:5, 386–97.

Coopersmith, Stanley, 1967. *The Antecedents of Self-Esteem.* San Francisco: W. H. Freeman and Company.

Davis, O. L., Jr., and B. R. Smoot, 1969. "Effects on the Verbal Teaching Behaviors of Beginning Secondary Teacher Candidates' Participation in a Program of Laboratory Teaching." Report Series No. 2, R & D Center for Teacher Education, The University of Texas at Austin.

Filson, T. N., 1957. "Factors Influencing the Level of Dependence in the Classroom." Unpublished doctoral dissertation, University of Minnesota.

Flanders, Ned A., 1969. "Teacher Effectiveness," in *Encyclopedia of Educational Research,* 4th Ed. New York: The Macmillan Company, p. 1429.

——— *et al.,* 1963. *Helping Teachers Change Their Behavior.* USOE Project Nos. 1721012 and 7-32-0560-171.0, University of Michigan.

Fuller, F. F., R. F. Peck, *et al.,* 1969. *Effects of Personalized Feedback During Teacher Preparation on Teacher Personality and Teaching Behavior.* Final Report, Project No. 5-0811, USOE Grant No. 3-10-032, R & D Report Series No. 4, The University of Texas at Austin.

Gallagher, James J., 1965. "Expressive Thought by Gifted Children on the Classroom." *Elementary English,* 42:559–68.

Gibb, L. M., and J. R. Gibb, 1952. "The Effects of the Use of 'Participative Action' Groups in a Course in General Psychology." *American Psychologist,* 7:247 (Abstract).

Heil, L. M., and C. Washburne, 1962. "Brooklyn College Research in Teacher Effectiveness." *Journal of Educational Research,* 55:347–51.

Johnston, Donald P., 1969. "Use of Selected Techniques for Supervising Student Teachers." USOE Project No. 8-D-069, Memphis State University.

Kounin, Jacob, 1970. *Discipline and Group Management in Classroom.* New York: Holt, Rinehart, and Winston, Inc.

Kroeber, Theodore C., 1963. "The Coping Functions of the Ego Mechanisms," in *The Study of Lives,* R. L. White, ed. New York: Atherton Press.

Lazarus, Richard S., 1966. *Psychological Stress and the Coping Process.* New York: McGraw-Hill Book Company.

Maltzman, I., 1960. "On the Training of Originality." *Psychological Review,* 67: 229–42.

Maslow, A. H., 1954. *Motivation and Personality.* New York: Harper and Row, Publishers, Inc.

McDonald, Frederick J., 1968. "Training Teachers as a Research Tool." Research Memo No. 24, Stanford Center for R & D in Teaching.

McKeachie, W. J., 1963. "Research on Teaching at the College and University Level," in *Handbook of Research on Teaching,* N. L. Gage, ed. Chicago: Rand McNally and Co.

Medley, Donald M., 1970. "The Language of Teacher Behavior," in *The Assessment Revolution.* Buffalo: State University College, Teacher Learning Center (1970).

Miller, George L., 1964. "An Investigation of Teaching Behavior and Pupil Thinking." Department of Education, University of Utah.

Morse, Kevin R., and O. L. Davis, Jr., 1970. "The Effectiveness of Teaching Laboratory Instruction on the Questioning Behaviors of Beginning Teacher Candidates." Report Series No. 43, R & D Center for Teacher Education, The University of Texas at Austin.

Morse, Kevin R., Marcella Kysilka, and O. L. Davis, Jr., 1969. "Effects of Different Types of Supervisory Feedback on Teacher Candidates' Development of Refocusing Behaviors." Report Series No. 48, R & D Center for Teacher Education, The University of Texas at Austin.

Murphy, Lois B., 1962. *The Widening World of Childhood.* New York: Basic Books, Inc.

Nicholsen, P. J., III, 1959. "An Experimental Investigation of the Effects of Training upon Creativity." Unpublished doctoral dissertation, University of Houston.

Ojemann, Ralph H., 1962. "The Significance of Education on Human Behavior for the Social Development of Children." *International Review of Education,* 8:61–73.

Orme, Michael E. J., and Richard F. Purnell, 1968. "Behavior Modification and Transfer in an Out-of-Control Classroom." Monograph No. 5, Center for R & D on Educational Differences, Harvard University.

Pankratz, Roger, 1967. "Verbal Interaction Patterns in the Classrooms of Selected Physics Teachers," in *Interaction Analysis: Theory, Research and Application,* E. J. Amidon and J. B. Hough, eds. Reading, Mass.: Addison-Wesley.

Peck, Robert F., 1965. "Coping Styles and Achievement: A Cross-National Study of School Children." USOE Grant No. 5–85–063. Austin: University of Texas Personality Research Center.

Prescott, Daniel, 1945. *Helping Teachers Understand Children.* Washington: American Council on Education.

Salomon, Gavriel, and Frederick J. McDonald, 1969. "Pre- and Post-Test Reactions to Self-Viewing One's Teaching Performance on Videotape." R & D Memo No. 44, Stanford Center for R & D in Teaching.

Sandefur, J. T., 1967. "An Experimental Study of Professional Education for Secondary Teachers." USOE Cooperative Research Project No. 2897, Kansas State Teachers College, Emporia.

———, R. Pankratz, and J. Sullivan, 1969. "Teaching Experience as a Modifier of Teaching Behavior." USOE Grant No. 68–008027–0010 (057), Kansas State Teachers College, Emporia.

Smith, B. O., 1969a. "Discipline," in *Encyclopedia of Educational Research,* 4th Ed. New York: The Macmillan Company.

———, 1969b. *Teachers for the Real World.* Washington: American Association of Colleges for Teacher Education.

Spaulding, R. L., 1966. "A Coping Analysis Schedule for Educational Settings (CASES)." Education Improvement Program, Duke University, Durham, North Carolina.

Sturgis, H. W., 1958. "The Relationship of the Teacher's Knowledge of the Student's Background to the Effectiveness of Teaching." Unpublished doctoral dissertation, New York University (*Dissertation Abstracts,* 1959, 19:11).

Susskind, Edwin C., 1969. "The Role of Question-Asking in the Elementary School Classroom," in *The Psycho-Educational Clinic.* Massachusetts Department of Mental Health Monograph #4.

Torrance, E. Paul, 1965. *Constructive Behavior.* Belmont, Calif.: Wadsworth Publishing Company.

6

Shaping Teachers' Attitudes

M. RAY LOREE

What constitutes research on the shaping of teachers' attitudes? Clearly such research includes experiments in which teachers or teachers-in-training are the subjects and an effort is made to learn something about the process through which the attitudes of teachers are changed. Relevant also are studies reporting efforts to develop techniques for measuring or assessing teachers' attitudes. A research gap is located when we compare a list of teachers' attitudes currently receiving research attention and the much longer list of attitudes included in statements of objectives of existing or proposed programs in teacher education. For the purpose of exploring possible directions for future attitudinal research in teacher education, it becomes desirable in defining a research area to leave room for the filling in of gaps that exist in current research. With this in mind we may delineate a field of research on shaping teachers' attitudes by seeking answers to four questions:

1. What attitudes are included in statements of objectives for teacher training programs?
2. What measurement approaches are currently used in research on teachers' attitudes?
3. What teachers' attitudes are related to teacher effectiveness?
4. What procedures designed to change teachers' attitudes have been tried in research settings?

Hopefully, a field of research—or at least a mini-field—can be sketched in the process of seeking answers to these four questions.

ATTITUDINAL OBJECTIVES IN TEACHER EDUCATION PROGRAMS

It is necessary to make a number of assumptions in order to justify the inclusion in a teacher training program of any educational objective involving the shaping of attitudes. First, it must be assumed that the attitude identified in the objective is one that facilitates the acquisition of teaching competencies and/or is characteristic of the "good teacher." Second, it must be assumed that at least some of the prospective teachers do not have the desired attitude on entering the teacher training program. And third, it must be assumed that it is possible to develop in the teacher the attitude identified in the objective.

The problem of identifying attitudes related to teaching competencies is complicated by the fact that teaching effectiveness is not a clearly defined quality. It is difficult to disagree with the conclusion reached by Rabinowitz and Travers (1953) that: "There is no way to discover effective and ineffective teachers unless one has made or is prepared to make a value judgment." Differences in value judgments can lead to different definitions of teaching effectiveness. An educator who believes that the teaching of factual subject matter is the most important function of a school is likely to arrive at a different definition of teaching competency than an educator who believes that the development of social and emotional security for pupils is the most important function. A diversity of opinion exists concerning the worth of many educational goals and practices.

Yet there is some agreement on what constitutes effective teaching. Most educators would agree that at least a part of what is meant by teaching competency is demonstrated when a teacher generates in her pupils an enthusiasm for learning, selects and sequences learning experiences appropriate to the readiness levels of her pupils, and is able to plan and implement procedures for evaluating learning. Thus, while it is possible to identify numerous points of disagreement among educators concerning the teaching-learning process, it is also possible to identify points of agreement. A survey of current efforts to rethink teacher education programs reveals differences in emphases more than outright disagreements concerning what attitudes of students should be shaped in a training program.

Three types of attitudinal change keep recurring in statements on recent efforts to rethink the objectives for teacher education programs. The first type of attitudinal change concerns the attitude of the teacher toward herself. Somehow the teacher education program is expected to lead the teacher to a better understanding of her own assets, beliefs, and values, and to help the teacher steadily improve her competencies. Thus, included in the University of Georgia Model Program are the affective domain objectives:

3.25.01. To develop and accept an accurate perception of self, in order to achieve a more adequate personality.
3.25.01.02. To assess the limits of one's potential in order to learn the extent of one's own capacities.
3.25.02. To acknowledge and accept one's social, psychological, and physical needs . . .
3.25.03. To acknowledge, accept, and deal with one's emotions, feelings, and intuitions . . .
3.25.06. To awaken to and develop an awareness of the process of becoming in order to achieve a more adequate personality [Johnson, Shearron, and Stauffer, 1969, pp. 118–22].

The University of Pittsburgh Model of Teacher Training contains a "guidance component" involving group process experiences, individual counseling, and group directing. Self-realization, self-development, and self-evaluation are identified as major goals for the guidance component of the Pittsburgh Model (Gorman, 1969).

The Syracuse Model, too, directs attention to the development of the teacher as an individual. The program is described by Hough (1968) as highly "process-oriented" with one focus on "the process of becoming more aware of self, self as a teacher interacting with children, and self as a teacher who is a member of an organization" (p. 48).

One of the goals the model program developed at the Research and Development Center for Teacher Education at the University of Texas is described by Fuller (1969a, p. 47) as:

> *Affective gain for teachers.* One expected outcome of a personalized program is self-actualized teachers, teachers who are able to benefit from education, who have a realistic view of their own behavior, who solve their own personal problems that may interfere with pupil learning, who adapt creatively to change, who are expert interactors; specifically teachers who are comfortable, aware, receptive, responsive, imaginative, committed and organized and who produce affective gain in students.

A second type of attitudinal objective stressed in teacher education programs is concerned with human relationships. Allen and Cooper (1969) in describing the Massachusetts Model Elementary Teacher Education Program include *warmth* and *consciousness of cultural differences* as desirable characteristics for elementary teachers. However, such concepts are defined in behavioral terms and specified "so that it is possible to teach these behaviors directly. . . ." This is a bit puzzling. One wonders whether "warmth" is to be defined behaviorally as it is manifested by a Hollywood actor's agent or as manifested by a midwestern farmer. The quality "warmth" is manifested differently by different people. And it is possible that what is related to teaching effectiveness is the *perception* of warmth by the pupil rather than a set of specified physical and verbal responses by the teacher.

A number of items in the Minnesota Teacher Attitude Inventory (MTAI) are concerned with teacher-pupil relationships. Additional items seem to test the teacher's understanding of child behavior. The notion that the teacher who understands children will be better able to empathize with them appears to be implicit within the Minnesota Teacher Attitude Inventory. From this point of view, teacher characteristics such as *warmth, consciousness of cultural differences,* and *empathy* are developed as by-products for the teacher who has increased her understanding of children. The assumption is, of course, that beliefs and behaviors are highly correlated. There is some evidence of a relationship between teachers' beliefs and (1) the behavior of the teacher in the classroom, and (2) the behavior of students in the classroom (see, for example, a study reported by Harvey *et al.*, 1968). However, there remains much to be learned concerning the conditions under which behaviors and beliefs correspond.

A third type of attitudinal objective is concerned with the *teaching-learning process.* Attitudinal objectives involving a generalized set toward the task of teaching are included in some teacher education programs. For example, Allen and Cooper (1969) report the development of "critical thinking" and "openness" as objectives included in the Massachusetts Model Elementary Teacher Education Program. The term *clinical behavior style* is used to denote an important objective within the Michigan State Model Program. Ivey and Houston (1969) explain the objective thus:

> . . . The term, clinical behavior style, denotes the particular and stylized set of behaviors and mental processes of a practitioner who has been specifically trained to utilize his client-related experience as a continuing learning experience through which to improve his professional skills and increase his knowledge. The clinical behavior style appropriate for a professional teacher consists of six phases: describing, analyzing, hypothesizing, prescribing, treating, and observing and evaluating consequences. The last activity, observing and evaluating consequences of the treatment administered, in turn leads to the first, describing the changed situation, to begin a recycling of feedback [p. 37].

The clinical behavior style portrayed in the Michigan program contrasts sharply with the teaching style portrayed by Jackson (1968) in his study of fifty elementary teachers who had been identified by their administrative superiors as "outstanding" teachers. For these teachers interviewed by Jackson, evidence of good teaching could be detected by the expressions on pupils' faces or by the willingness of pupils to work above and beyond minimal expectations. Tests were distrusted as evidence that pupils were learning. Teachers formed judgments concerning satisfactory learning progress on the basis of more than one thousand daily pupil-teacher interactions. A technical vocabulary unique to teaching was noticeably absent as the teachers discussed their work. The teachers' talk was marked by its conceptual simplicity. Jackson (1968) elaborates:

> Four aspects of the conceptual simplicity revealed in teachers' language are worthy of comment. These are: (1) an uncomplicated view of causality; (2) an intuitive rather than rational approach to classroom events; (3) an opinionated, as opposed to an open-minded stance when confronted with alternative teaching practices; and (4) a narrowness in the working definitions assigned to abstract terms [p. 144].

Teacher education programs may attempt to persuade teachers to subscribe to certain beliefs about the teaching-learning process as well as to develop generalized teaching styles. Such emotionally loaded terms as *democratic* versus *authoritarian, learner-centered* versus *teacher-centered* appear designed to help the student to believe that one teaching style is right and another is wrong.

In summary, three types of attitudinal objectives keep recurring in statements on teacher education programs. Objectives may be concerned with the teacher's attitude toward: (1) herself; (2) her pupils; or (3) the teaching-learning process. It is not always clear whether the stated objective is focused primarily upon (1) a change in the belief of the teacher; (2) a change in the feelings of the teacher; (3) a change in the behavior of the teacher; or (4) all of the foregoing.

We turn now to problems of measurement that are encountered in research in teachers' attitudes.

ASSESSING TEACHERS' ATTITUDES

Scott (1968), in reviewing the current status of attitude measurement, points out that the construct *attitude* has become so complex that one can no longer talk clearly about "measuring an attitude." What is done is to use procedures to measure a particular property of an attitude.

It is convenient to discuss past and current attempts to assess teachers' attitudes under four headings: (1) self-reporting inventories; (2) systematic observation; (3) projective techniques; and (4) the semantic differential. Each of these approaches to the assessment of attitudes reflects varying meanings in what is considered to be the central core of meaning for the term "attitude." Or, viewed in another way, each approach poses a different set of problems in making inferences from objective data to the construct that is to be measured.

1. SELF-REPORTING INVENTORIES Self-reporting inventories designed to assess attitudes often take the form of a number of statements that constitute beliefs or feelings on a subject. The individual tested reports the extent of his agreement or disagreement to each statement. The most widely used instrument for the measurement of teacher attitudes has been the Minnesota Teacher Attitude Inventory (MTAI). This instrument "is designed to measure those attitudes of a teacher which predict how well he will get along with pupils in interpersonal relationships, and indirectly how well satisfied he will be with teaching as a vocation" (Cook, Leeds, and Callis, 1951, p. 3).

One limitation of self-reporting inventories is that a person's behavior and his belief statements may not correspond. The teacher who is very restrictive may report that children should be allowed more freedom in the classroom. There is the possibility that a teacher who gets along poorly with her pupils may score high on the MTAI. Hence validity studies for self-reporting inventories may appropriately take the form of investigating the correspondence between beliefs and behaviors. Getzels and Jackson (1963) have reviewed the procedures followed in constructing and validating the MTAI and describe subsequent validity studies. There is some evidence that teachers who are rated superior by their supervisors, their pupils, and by competent observers tend to obtain higher MTAI scores than teachers less highly regarded. A number of studies relate MTAI scores to a variety of teacher characteristics. For example, as one might expect, females tend to score higher than males; elementary teachers higher than high school teachers; teachers who gave few failing grades scored higher than teachers who gave many failing grades; and teachers who were liked by their pupils tended to score higher than teachers who were disliked. In one interesting study Della Piana and Gage (1955) investigated the hypothesis that pupils' liking of teachers is a function of the interaction between pupil values and teacher attitudes. These investigators identified certain classes in which the children valued teachers who were effective in helping them achieve intellectual objectives (i.e., a cognitive orientation). For these classes, MTAI scores correlated only .05 with pupil ratings of teachers. Among classes who valued teachers who were effective in helping pupils satisfy their emotional social needs (i.e., an affective orientation), MTAI scores correlated .57 with pupil ratings of teachers.

The MTAI yields a single score that is thought to distinguish effective from ineffective teachers. An alternative strategy is exemplified by the scale developed by Wehling and Charters (1969) to measure teachers' beliefs about the teaching process. Teachers' attitudes are considered by these investigators to be most meaningfully described as a complex organization of beliefs. Evolving out of a number of questionnaires and factor analytic studies, questionnaire items associated with eight dimensions of teacher conceptions of the educative process were developed. The eight dimensions and the central theme for each dimension are as follows:

Dimension	*Theme*
1. Subject Matter Emphasis	It is important that children learn subject matter in school.
2. Personal Adjustment Idealogy	The social-emotional needs of pupils are important.
3. Student Autonomy vs. Teacher Direction	Give children more freedom vs. Keep pupils busy with a well-planned program.
4. Emotional Disengagement	Keep proper "professional distance" from pupils.
5. Consideration of Student Viewpoint	Understand and love your pupils.
6. Classroom Order	Keep firm control of your class.
7. Student Challenge	Challenge students with difficult learning tasks.
8. Integrative Learning	Teach the interrelationships of knowledge.

No effort is made by Wehling and Charters to relate their scale to teacher effectiveness. Conceivably, many patterns of scores of "effective teachers" could emerge.

Factor analytic studies based on ratings of teachers as well as scores on attitude inventories have identified different dimensions of teachers' attitudes. Studies by Kerlinger (1956, 1958, 1966) identify two factors—progressivism and traditionalism—that underlie attitudes toward education. Sontag (1968) presents evidence indicating that for both elementary and secondary teachers this basic progressivism vs. traditionalism attitudinal orientation influences judgments on the relative importance of a wide range of teacher competencies. Horn and Morrison (1965) reported a factor analytic study in which five factors were found in the MTAI. A factor consisting of seventeen items and labeled "Traditionalism vs. Modern Beliefs about Child Control" turned out to make the greatest common variance contribution. A study reported by Harvey and his associates (1968) points to a relationship between teachers' beliefs and (1) the behavior of the teacher in the classroom and (2) the behavior of students in the classroom. Teachers were classified as *abstract* or *concrete* on the basis of written statements expressing beliefs about "religion," "friendship," "the American way of life," "sin," "education," "the family," and "sex." Concrete teachers were found to be less resourceful, more dictatorial, and more punitive in the classroom than were abstract teachers. The students of abstract teachers were found to be more involved, more active, higher in achievement, and less concrete than were the students of concrete teachers.

2. SYSTEMATIC OBSERVATION In discussing measurement applications in teacher education, Ebel (1966) observes that:

> Research on measurement applications in teacher education has been dominated by the search for valid measures of teacher personality. . . . Eventually, I predict, research on the human interpersonal dimension of teacher effectiveness will turn away from paper-and-pencil tests of personality toward refinement of techniques for observing the prospective teacher's actual behavior and describing the observations concisely and meaningfully [p. 20].

Weick (1968) has surveyed the status and problems of systematic observational methods. Medley and Mitzel (1963) discuss the problem of measuring classroom behavior by systematic observation and describe a number of devices that have been developed. Withall's (1949) measure of classroom climate, the Teacher Characteristic Study of Ryans (1960), the categories developed by Anderson and Brewer (1945) to differentiate dominative from integrative teacher contacts with pupils, the behavior categories developed by Flanders (1960) for analyzing student-teacher interactions, the categories developed by Meux and Smith (1964) to analyze the verbal behavior of teachers and students, the Observation Schedule and Record (OScAR) developed by Medley and Mitzel (1958), and the Fuller Affective Interaction Records (FAIR) developed by Fuller (1969b)—represent a few of the efforts to systematize observations of teachers and students in the classroom.

Of the observational schedules referred to above, Fuller's schedule FAIR focuses most directly upon the measurement of attitudinal objectives of a teacher education program. In one form of this schedule, observations of teacher-pupil interactions are made along five dimensions: (1) *responsiveness* —responds or initiates; (2) *approval*—approves or is noncommital or disapproves; (3) *inclusion*—invites or excludes; (4) *control*—permitting or restricting; and (5) *self-other*—orientation toward self or others. By combining certain dimensions, fourteen teacher categories and fourteen student categories plus five categories for other eventualities are generated. For example, a teacher's response indicative of sharing a feeling with a student involves a combination of responding, approval, inviting, permitting, orientation toward others. Electronic and mechanical equipment is used to aid an observer code and analyze a videotape of a classroom in action. Interjudge reliability studies indicate that for most of the teacher and student categories agreement between trained judges is good.

Systematic observation is facilitated by the use of categories when the categories are well defined and relevant to the problem under investigation. Rating scales often are used when observation is less systematic and when the categories of behavior are broader and involve a higher degree of inference on the part of the observer. For some research purposes, a rating scale may yield sufficiently precise measurements. Harvey and others (1966, 1968) have used rating scales to assess teachers' overt resourcefulness, dictatorialness, and punitiveness. Remmers (1963) has discussed the problems involved in using rating methods for research purposes.

3. PROJECTIVE TECHNIQUES Personality questionnaires, although objective and economical, are limited with respect to the amount of information they can yield. On the other hand, projective instruments can yield a rich variety of information but are difficult to objectify without sacrificing much of the richness of the data. Getzels and Jackson (1963) have reviewed the literature on the use of projective techniques in the analysis of teacher personality.

Over a period of years, researchers from the University of Texas have been experimenting with automated personality assessment of teachers using projective test data (Peck, 1960; Peck, Bown, and Veldman, 1964; Veldman, 1967; Veldman, Menaker, and Williams, 1967). One of the instruments developed—the Peck-Veldman One-Word Sentence Completion test (OWSC)—consists of ninety stems (e.g., "Bosses are . . ."). A subject is instructed to respond to each stem with no more than one word. In developing an automated scoring system for the OWSC, the responses of one thousand female sophomores were punched on tab cards and transferred to magnetic tape. Compiling programs were written to produce a series of listings of completions—one listing for each item. The resulting response banks were used to compile a "dictionary" for the computer to use in scoring new OWSC protocols. Twenty-five psychological variables were selected for rating from the OWSC data. A number of variables concern a subject's perception of self with respect to various personality characteristics, other variables concern attitudes toward others, and still other variables are relevant to role performance in a classroom. Correlations between the machine scores and the consensus ratings of two trained raters averaged .66 across the twenty-five variables and ranged from .45 to .94. Interrater reliability also was computed as .66 and ranged from .38 to .95. The OWSC is one of the instruments used by the Texas group in its effort to personalize and individualize a teacher education program.

Veldman's test of Directed Imagination is a second projective instrument developed at the University of Texas. The test is quite simple. Subjects are provided with four blank sheets and are instructed to: "Write four fictional stories about teachers and their experiences." Four minutes are allowed for each story. An extensive scoring manual has been developed based on a sample of 250 protocols provided by 125 female students (Veldman, Menaker, and Williams, 1967). Fifteen variables concerning structural, psychological, and educational aspects of the stories narrated were identified. Internal consistency reliabilities have been reported to range between .53 and .82. Four construct validity studies have yielded promising findings (Veldman and Menaker, 1969).

4. THE SEMANTIC DIFFERENTIAL The semantic differential has become one of the standard tools of attitude studies and has particular merit when the researcher wishes to measure unconscious shifts occurring in the con-

notations attached to an attitude object. A semantic differential consists of seven-unit scales, with pairs of adjectives opposite in meaning placed at each end of a scale (e.g., *good* —/—/—/—/—/—/—/ *bad*). A subject is asked to judge a concept (such as *teacher*) against the series of scales. One cluster of scales consists of pairs of adjectives that are *evaluative* (e.g., good-bad, pleasant-unpleasant, valuable-worthless). A second cluster has adjectives concerned with *potency* (e.g., strong-weak, heavy-light). A third cluster contains pairs of adjectives contrasting *activity* levels (e.g., fast-slow, active-passive).

The semantic differential would seem to be a useful instrument to measure shifts in attitudes of subjects while experiencing contact with persons of a different subculture. Mazer (1969), using semantic differentials, found that student teachers evaluated disadvantaged children more favorably after an instructional program consisting of both didactic and contact experiences. Butts and Raun (1968a,b) have used semantic differentials to measure shifts in the attitudes of students toward sciences, toward teaching, and toward an innovative program in science.

TEACHER ATTITUDES RELATED TO EFFECTIVENESS

One difficulty in identifying which teacher attitudes are related to teacher effectiveness is the lack of agreement as to what constitutes teacher effectiveness (Biddle, 1964). Yet there is not total disagreement. Most teacher educators would agree that the effective teacher is "fair" to her pupils, is "flexible" in adapting teaching objectives to the needs of pupils, and "respects the individuality" of each pupil.

Research that is designed to investigate whether there are identifiable teachers' *attitudes* that help to explain and predict desirable teachers' behaviors may have implications for teacher training programs. A study reported by Sprinthall, Whiteley, and Mosher (1966) is illustrative. The findings of this research support the hypothesis that cognitive flexibility (an attitude) and effective teaching (behavior) are related. Apprentice teachers with open flexible systems (as measured by the Rorschach and an adaptation of the Thematic Apperception Test) were observed and rated as more effective than apprentice teachers who previously had been identified as rigid. Effectiveness was rated in this study on the basis of the observed ability of the apprentice teachers to plan under stress, to be responsive to the learning needs of pupils, and to show flexibility in implementing instructional plans.

A second type of research that has implications for teacher education programs investigates the effects of the behavioral manifestation of an attitude by a teacher on the learning of pupils. For example, Rosenshine (1969) reviews research on the effects of teachers' enthusiastic and animated behaviors on pupil achievement. The evidence indicates "that ratings given to teachers on such behaviors as 'stimulating,' 'energetic,' 'mobile,' 'enthusiastic,' and 'animated' are related to measures of pupil achievement" (p. 15).

SHAPING TEACHERS' ATTITUDES

To what extent is it possible to modify the types of attitudes that are incorporated within attitudinal objectives of current teacher education programs? Two sources of information are relevant to this question: (1) reports on experimental efforts to shape teachers' attitudes; and (2) the literature on attitude formation in the field of social psychology. Both of these sources will be utilized as we look at two approaches to the problem of changing the attitudes of teachers. In the first approach, the student teacher is provided with information. This information may be imparted through a variety of media—lectures, readings, television, films, demonstrations, etc. The newly acquired information is expected to change the belief system of the learner. In the second approach, the student teacher is provided with experiences in working with children, such as in a student teaching assignment. A change in attitude is expected to emerge out of the effort of the learner to cope with his learning task.

Changing Attitudes through Information Input

Several studies have demonstrated that it is possible to modify the belief system of teachers through course work. Leton (1961), for example, reported that the attitudes toward children of elementary education students became significantly more favorable during a course in child development. Three methods of college teaching (lecture, case-centered, and group-centered) were used for three randomly selected classes of elementary education students. Students were pre- and post-tested on the MTAI and the Schoben Parent Attitude Survey. The attitudes of the students toward children, as measured by these tests, improved under each method of instruction. The amount of attitude change was not related to teaching method.

Cummins (1961) has reported a study in which the orientation of teacher candidates toward teaching became increasingly similar to that of their instructors during a four-year teacher training program. The teacher candidates at Arkansas A & M College were administered a fifty-one item Teacher Role Sort. This instrument contains statements representing a continuum of teaching biases ranging from "freeing" and "guiding" to "molding" concepts of teaching. The A & M staff was reported as biased in favor of the freeing concept of teaching. Senior students, but not freshmen, were found to be similarly biased.

A number of studies report the effects of a teacher education program upon

MTAI scores. For example, Rocchio and Kearney (1956) found that teachers who had recently completed a course in mental hygiene scored higher on the MTAI than teachers who had not recently taken such a course. Brim (1966) tested 250 undergraduate students in a teacher training program at the beginning and end of a fall quarter. The students were at various levels in their program. Significant gains occurred for the total group, and student means on the MTAI were higher at each successive level of the program.

Some caution is in order in interpreting the various studies reporting positive effects of teacher education programs upon MTAI scores. It may be that students in their teacher education program discover the beliefs of their instructors and their higher scores reflect their improved perception of "acceptable beliefs" rather than their own firmly held convictions. Rabinowitz (1954) and Polmantier and Ferguson (1960) have reported studies showing markedly altered scores on the MTAI when college students and teachers were given instructions to simulate the attitudinal orientations of particular types of teachers.

It is not surprising that college courses can affect changes in the beliefs of students. It has long been established that exposure to information can serve to form or to alter attitudes *under certain conditions*. Change is facilitated when the source of information is respected, when the initial attitude is not firmly entrenched, when the communication reflects attitudes that are consistent to the needs of the receiver, and when the communication is acceptable to important reference groups of the receiver. Possibly most, if not all, of these conditions often are fairly well met in courses offered to students in a teacher education program.

Student teaching is generally regarded as a highly significant aspect of a teacher preparation program. Because of the central role played by the cooperating teacher in guiding student teaching experiences, it seems reasonable to hypothesize that cooperating teachers will influence the attitudes and behavior of student teachers. This influence may occur because the cooperating teacher is a source of information to the student teacher. Or possibly the student teacher may acquire the attitudes of the cooperating teacher through the process of identification. In either case, the cooperating teacher serves as a model for the student teacher. Yee (1969) has reviewed studies that test the hypothesis that cooperating teachers influence the attitudes and teaching behavior of their student teachers. In general, the hypothesis was supported. In his own study, Yee used a frequency-of-change-in-product-moment technique to assess influence. A modified form of the MTAI was administered to student teachers and their cooperating teachers prior to and after student teaching experiences. An analysis of pre- and post-test scores of 124 teacher-student dyads (43 in elementary schools and 81 in secondary schools) indicated that most student teachers tended to shift in their attitudes toward those of their cooperating teachers. In some cases, however, the influence was negative. As one student teacher put it, "My cooperating teacher's attitude toward and rapport with pupils was so bad, I learned what not to do in classrooms" (p. 328).

Studies on the relationships between MTAI scores and teacher behavior have yielded discouraging results (Giebink, 1967). However this failure of the MTAI to predict teacher behavior is not really surprising. From reinforcement learning theory, one would expect the behavioral component of an attitude to be strengthened through reinforcement. Thus the teacher who believes that getting along with pupils is important would be likely to have this attitude strengthened when satisfying consequences resulted from her efforts to establish cooperative relationships with her pupils. One would predict a weakening of the attitude when undesirable consequences resulted from the teacher's efforts to get along with her pupils. But a high degree of skill is required in order to establish within a classroom the kind of interpersonal relationships that are conducive to efficient learning. Much more is involved in this skill than merely believing in the importance of getting along with pupils.

It would be a mistake to overgeneralize from studies reporting a poor relationship between attitude and behavior measures. Under certain conditions, attitude measures predict behavior fairly well. Gough, Durflinger, and Hill (1968) were able to predict teaching effectiveness from certain scales on the California Psychological Inventory. Silberman (1969) interviewed ten third-grade teachers to determine the pupils toward whom they held attitudes of attachment, concern, indifference, or rejection. Each of the grade three classrooms was observed in order to record the teacher's behavior toward these identified pupils. Teachers' attitudes in this study did find expression in their actions. However some attitudes were given clearer expression than others. Teachers evidently felt less constrained to express concern or indifference than to express rejection or attachment.

Changing Attitudes through Experiences

Conditioning concepts may be useful in explaining and predicting the attitudinal changes occurring as a result of certain experiences. An attitude elicits a feeling of pleasantness or unpleasantness. This feeling tone aspect of an attitude may be explained in terms of classical conditioning. The behavioral component of an attitude may be learned through instrumental conditioning. Hence it is relevant to ask two questions in order to predict the kinds of attitude changes that are likely to occur during student teaching or other experiences in working with children:

1. Was the experience pleasant or unpleasant?
2. What were the consequences of the student teacher's behaviors as she interacted with children?

Participation in student teaching may have an adverse effect on attitudes toward self and children (Walberg, 1966). When the teaching efforts of the student teacher are met with much less success than hoped for, the student teacher's self-esteem may suffer and the collective halos may be figuratively removed from atop the heads of her pupils. Bills, Macagnoni, and Elliott (1964) found significant negative changes in the *openness* of both elementary and secondary student teachers during their student teaching. The negative changes were greater for the student teachers who were initially more open. It is not clear at the present time whether the adverse effects on attitudes resulting from a teacher training experience persist over a long time period or whether the effects are merely of a temporary nature.

Apparently not all contacts of student teachers with boys and girls are traumatic. Favorable shifts may occur in the attitudes of student teachers as they learn a new responsible role in their interactions with children and youth. Nagle (1959) reports an improvement in attitudes of undergraduate teachers during their teaching experience. Cox (1960) compared the shifts in attitudes of two groups of students enrolled in a pre-student teaching course, Human Growth and Development. Members of the experimental group were provided with experiences in working with children and youth groups of a city. A control group did not have this experience as part of the course. Both groups gained significantly in their scores on the MTAI. However, the laboratory group did not significantly outgain the control group.

Mazer (1969) has reported a study on attitude and personality changes in student teachers of disadvantaged youth. The study consisted of two phases. The first 7½-week session consisted of didactic experiences (lectures and reading) plus observation and participation (at the planning level) of work carried on by professionals in poverty stricken areas and in guidance clinics, detention homes, and community centers. In the second 7½-week session, students participated either at a summer camp serving disadvantaged youth or at an elementary school where they were assigned to recruit children of migrant families for summer educational programs. Semantic differential scales were used to assess attitude shifts and were administered at the beginning, after seven weeks, and at the end of the program. During the course of the fifteen-week program, rather substantial favorable shifts were noted in the attitudes of student teachers toward disadvantaged children and the parents of disadvantaged children.

Studies are lacking in which systematic observation is used to assess the effects of experiences on attitudes. Yet it is the behavioral component of an attitude that is of prime concern for many attitudinal objectives in teacher education. We do have studies reported in which learning experiences are designed to shape the behavioral component of an attitude. Joyce and Hodges (1966), for example, reported an instructional procedure designed to increase teaching flexibility. But we do not have concomitant efforts to measure, through systematic observation, the behavioral manifestations of a belief in the importance of flexibility—i.e., a belief that more efficient learning becomes possible when a teacher can purposefully exhibit a wide range of teaching styles. Yet it may be that, for certain attitudinal objectives in teacher education programs, instructional procedures should be directed toward shaping both the belief and the behavioral components of an attitude. Thus, with respect to teacher flexibility, it seems reasonable to expect that:

1. A teacher who believes that more efficient learning becomes possible when a teacher can purposefully exhibit a wide range of teaching styles will attempt to vary her style;
2. When the teacher's attempts to vary her teaching style are followed by favorable consequences (e.g., her students learn more), the favorable attitude toward flexibility will be strengthened;
3. The teacher who has received flexibility training—i.e., the teacher who has learned efficient ways of adapting her teaching style to the demands of the teaching situation—is more apt to be successful in her efforts to vary her style of teaching and hence more likely to experience favorable consequences from her efforts.

Research Gaps

Of the types of attitudinal changes emphasized in recent statements of objectives for teacher education programs, objectives concerned with human relationships have received the most research emphasis. With a few notable exceptions, researchers have not directed and sustained their attention to the study of changes, within a teacher education context, in the attitudes of the teacher candidate toward herself. Although some effort recently has been made to study the beliefs of teachers respecting the teaching-learning process, no research attention has been devoted to finding ways of inducing in teachers a scientific orientation to their work. However, as previously noted, an important objective in the Michigan State Model Program was the development in teachers of a *clinical behavior style*—which is defined as consisting of six phases: describing, analyzing, hypothesizing, prescribing, treating, and observing and evaluating consequences.

In recent years there has been an increase in the diversity of measurement tools used in research on ways of changing teachers' attitudes. There remains, however, much reliance on self-reporting inventories such as the MTAI even when behavioral changes, rather than belief changes, are of primary importance. It is not defensible to assume that measures of beliefs and behaviors are inevitably highly correlated, particularly when the behaviors constitute complex skills. Techniques for measuring classroom behavior are available. It remains only to apply the techniques more extensively in research on shaping teachers' attitudes.

In reviewing research on instructional methods of shaping teachers' attitudes, one does not find efforts to apply consistency theory approaches to attitude change. Analyses of the history and current status of consistency theories may be found in McGuire (1966, 1969), Zajonc (1968), and Sears and Abeles (1969). The basic notion of the consistency theory approach to changing attitudes is that a person strives to maintain harmony (1) within his belief system, and (2) between his beliefs and his overt behavior—and will adjust his attitudes and behavior in order to achieve consistency. An instructional effort to stimulate students to examine the underlying assumptions and the implications of various positions on controversial issues represents one type of application of consistency theory to attitude change. Doubtlessly, many instructors within teacher education programs strive to stimulate their students to examine critically the many sides of a controversial issue. And to stimulate thinking, an instructor may present points of view that he feels are contrary to the beliefs of his students. However, research is lacking on factors affecting the effectiveness of instructional procedures in which consistency theory approaches are applied for the purpose of shaping teachers' attitudes.

REFERENCES

Allen, D. W., and J. M. Cooper, 1969. "Massachusetts Model Elementary Teacher Education Program." *Journal of Research and Development in Education,* 21:31–35.

Anderson, H. H., and H. M. Brewer, 1945. "Studies of Teachers' Classroom Personalities: I. Dominative and Socially Integrative Behavior of Kindergarten Teachers." *Applied Psychological Monographs,* No. 6.

Biddle, B. J., 1964. "The Integration of Teacher Effectiveness Research, in *Contemporary Research on Teacher Effectiveness,* B. J. Biddle and W. J. Ellena, eds. New York: Holt, Rinehart and Winston, Inc., pp. 1–40.

Bills, R. E., V. M. Macagnoni, and R. J. Elliott, 1964. *Student Teacher Personality Change as a Function of the Personalities of Supervising and Cooperating Teachers.* Cooperative Research Project No. S–020. University, Alabama: College of Education, University of Alabama.

Brim, B. J., 1966. "Attitude Changes in Teacher Education Students." *Journal of Educational Research,* 59:441–45.

Butts, D. P., and C. E. Raun, 1968a. *A Study in Teacher Attitude Change.* Austin, Texas: The Research Development Center for Teacher Education.

———, 1968b. *A Study of Teacher Change.* Austin, Texas: The Research Development for Teacher Education.

Cook, W. W., C. H. Leeds, and R. Callis, 1951. *Minnesota Teacher Attitude Inventory*. New York: Psychological Corporation.

Cox, D., 1960. "An Objective and Empirical Study of the Factors of Laboratory Experience in a Professional Education Course Prior to Student Teaching." *Journal of Experimental Education,* 29:89–94.

Cummins, R. E., 1961. "Role Study in Teacher Training: A Sequel." *Journal of Educational Sociology,* 35:119–20.

Della Piana, G. M., and N. L. Gage, 1955. "Pupils' Values and the Validity of the Minnesota Teacher Attitude Inventory." *Journal of Educational Psychology,* 46:167–78.

Ebel, R. L., 1966. "Measurement Applications in Teacher Education: A Review of Relevant Research." *Journal of Teacher Education,* 17:15–25.

Fiske, D. W., and P. H. Pearson, 1970. "Theories and Techniques of Personality Measurement," in *Annual Review of Psychology,* P. H. Mussen and M. R. Rosenzweig, eds. Palo Alto: Annual Reviews, Inc., Volume 21, pp. 49–86.

Flanders, N. A., 1960. *Teacher Influence, Pupil Attitudes and Achievement: Studies in Interaction Analysis.* Final Report, Cooperative Research Project No. 397, Minneapolis: University of Minnesota.

Fuller, Frances F., 1969a. "Personalization (Module Building)," in 1969 *Annual Report of Research and Development in Education.* Austin, Texas: The Research and Development Center for Teacher Education, pp. 46–75.

———, 1969b. *FAIR System Manual. Fuller Affective Interaction Records.* Austin, Texas: The Research Development Center for Teacher Education.

Getzels, J. W., and P. W. Jackson, 1963. "The Teacher's Personality and Characteristics," in *The Handbook of Research on Teaching,* N. L. Gage, ed. Chicago: Rand McNally and Co., pp. 506–82.

Giebink, J. W., 1967. "A Failure of the Minnesota Teacher Attitude Inventory to Relate to Teacher Behavior." *Journal of Teacher Education,* 18:233–39.

Gorman, C. J., 1969. "The University of Pittsburgh Model of Teacher Training for the Individualization of Instruction." *Journal of Research and Development in Education,* 2:44–46.

Gough, H. G., G. W. Durflinger, and R. E. Hill, 1968. "Predicting Performance in Student Teaching from the California Psychological Inventory." *Journal of Educational Psychology,* 59:119–27.

Harvey, O. J., M. Prather, B. J. White, and J. K. Hoffmeister, 1968. "Teachers' Beliefs, Classroom Atmosphere and Student Behavior." *American Educational Research Journal,* 5:151–66.

Harvey, O. J., B. J. White, M. Prather, R. D. Alter, and J. K. Hoffmeister, 1966. "Teacher's Belief Systems and Preschool Atmospheres." *Journal of Educational Psychology,* 57:373–81.

Horn, J. L., and W. E. Morrison, 1965. "Dimensions of Teacher Attitudes." *Journal of Educational Psychology,* 56:118–25.

Hough, J., 1968. *Specifications for a Comprehensive Undergraduate and Inservice*

Teacher Education Program for Elementary Teachers. Washington, D.C.: USOE Bureau of Research, U.S. Government Printing Office, FS 5.258: 58016.

Ivey, J. E., Jr., and W. R. Houston, 1969. "Behavioral Science Elementary Teacher Education Program." *Journal of Research and Development in Education,* 2:36–39.

Jackson, P. W., 1968. *Life in Classrooms.* New York: Holt, Rinehart, and Winston, Inc.

Johnson, C. E., G. F. Shearron, A. J. Stauffer, 1969. "Georgia Education Model Specifications for the Preparation of Elementary Teachers—A Summary." *Journal of Research and Development in Education,* 2:52–135.

Joyce, B. R., and R. E. Hodges, 1966. "Instructional Flexibility Training." *Journal of Teacher Education,* 17:409–16.

Kerlinger, F., 1956. "The Attitude Structure of the Individual: A Q Study of the Educational Attitudes of Professors and Laymen." *Genetic Psychology Monographs,* 53:283–329.

———, 1958. "Progressivism and Traditionalism: Basic Factors of Educational Attitudes." *Journal of Social Psychology,* 48:111–35.

———, 1966. "Attitudes toward Education and Perception of Teacher Characteristics: A Q Study." *American Educational Research Journal,* 3:159–68.

Leton, D. A., 1961. "An Evaluation of Course Methods in Teaching Child Development." *Journal of Educational Research,* 35:118–22.

McGuire, W. J., 1966. "The Current Status of Cognitive Consistency Theories," in *Cognitive Consistency: Motivational Antecedents and Behavioral Consequents,* S. Feldman, ed. New York: Academic Press, pp. 1–46.

———, 1969. "The Nature of Attitudes and Attitude Change," in *The Handbook of Social Psychology,* G. Lindzey and E. Aronson, eds. 2nd ed. Reading, Mass.: Addison-Wesley Publishing Company, Vol. 3, pp. 136–314.

Mazer, G. E., 1969. "Attitude and Personality Change in Student Teachers of Disadvantaged Youth." *Journal of Educational Research,* 63:116–20.

Medley, D. M., and H. E. Mitzel, 1958. " A Technique for Measuring Classroom Behavior." *Journal of Educational Psychology,* 49:86–92.

———, 1963. "Measuring Classroom Behavior by Systematic Observation," in *Handbook of Research on Teaching,* N. L. Gage, ed. Chicago: Rand McNally and Co., pp. 247–328.

Meux, M., and B. O. Smith, 1964. "Logical Dimensions of Teacher Behavior," in *Contemporary Research on Teacher Effectiveness,* B. J. Biddle and W. J. Ellena, eds. New York: Holt, Rinehart, and Winston, Inc., 127–64.

Nagle, L. M., 1959. "Some Effects of Student Teaching Patterns upon Professional Attitudes." *Journal of Educational Research,* 52:355–57.

Peck, R. F., 1960. "Personality Patterns of Prospective Teachers." *Journal of Experimental Education,* 29:169–75.

———, O. H. Bown, and D. J. Veldman, 1964. "Mental Health in Teacher Education." *Journal of Teacher Education,* 15:319–27.

Polmantier, P. C., and J. L. Ferguson, 1960. "Faking the Minnesota Teacher Attitude Inventory." *Educational and Psychological Measurement,* 20:79–82.

Rabinowitz, W., 1954. "The Fakability of the Minnesota Teacher Attitude Inventory." *Educational and Psychological Measurement,* 14:657–64.

———, and R. M. W. Travers, 1953. "Problems of Defining and Assessing Teacher Effectiveness." *Educational Theory,* 3:212–19.

Remmers, H. H., 1963. "Rating Methods in Research on Teaching," in *The Handbook of Research on Teaching,* N. L. Gage, ed. Chicago: Rand McNally and Co., pp. 329–78.

Rocchio, P. D., and N. C. Kearney, 1956. "Does a Course in Mental Hygiene Help Teachers?" *Understanding the Child,* 25:91–94.

Rosenshine, B., 1969. "Effects of Teacher's Enthusiastic and Animated Behaviors on Pupil Achievement: A Review of Research." Philadelphia: Temple University (Mimeo).

Ryans, D. G., 1960. *Characteristics of Teachers.* Washington, D. C.: American Council on Education.

Sandgren, D. L., and L. G. Schmidt, 1956. "Does Practice Teaching Change Aitttudes toward Teaching?" *Journal of Educational Research,* 49:673–80.

Scott, William A., 1968. "Attitude Measurement," in *The Handbook of Social Psychology,* G. Lindzey and E. Aronson, eds. 2nd ed. Reading, Mass.: Addison-Wesley Publishing Company, Vol. 2, pp. 204–73.

Sears, D. O., and R. P. Abeles, 1969. "Attitudes and Opinions," in *Annual Review of Psychology,* Volume 20, P. H. Mussen and M. R. Rosenzweig, eds. Palo Alto: Annual Reviews, Inc., pp. 253–88.

Silberman, M. L., 1969. "Behavioral Expression of Teachers' Attitudes toward Elementary School Students." *Journal of Educational Psychology,* 60:402–7.

Sontag, M., 1968. "Attitudes toward Education and Perceptions of Teacher Behavior." *American Educational Research Journal,* 5:385–402.

Sprinthall, N. A., J. M. Whiteley, and R. L. Mosher, 1966. "A Study of Teacher Effectiveness." *Journal of Teacher Education,* 17:93–106.

Veldman, D. J., 1967. "Computer-based Sentence Completion Interviews." *Journal of Consulting Psychology,* 14:153–57.

———, and S. L. Menaker, 1969. "The Directed Imagination Method for Projective Assessment of Teacher Candidates." *Journal of Educational Psychology,* 60:178–87.

———, S. L. Menaker, and D. L. Williams, 1967. *Manual for Scoring the Test of Directed Imagination.* Austin, Texas: The Research Development Center for Teacher Education.

Walberg, H. J., 1966. "Self-Conception in Beginning Teachers." *Journal of Teacher Education,* 17:254.

Wehling, L. J., and W. W. Charters, 1969. "Dimensions of Teacher Beliefs about the Teaching Process." *American Educational Research Journal,* 6: 7–30.

Weick, K. E., 1968. "Systematic Observational Methods," in *The Handbook of Social Psychology,* G. Lindzey and E. Aronson, eds. 2nd ed. Reading, Mass.: Addison-Wesley Publishing Company, Vol. 2, pp. 357–451.

Withall, J., 1949. "Development of a Technique for the Measurement of Socio-emotional Climates in Classrooms." *Journal of Experimental Education,* 17: 347–61.

Yee, A. H., 1969. "Do Cooperating Teachers Influence the Attitudes of Student Teachers?" *Journal of Educational Psychology,* 60:327–32.

Zajonc, R. B., 1968. "Cognitive Theories in Social Psychology," in *The Handbook of Social Psychology,* G. Lindzey and E. Aronson, eds. 2nd ed. Reading, Mass.: Addison-Wesley Publishing Company, Vol. 3, pp. 320–411.

7

Designs for Programs of Teacher Education

S. C. T. CLARKE

The preparation of teachers is logically determined by the nature of the teaching tasks for which they are being prepared. A conceptualization of teaching, conscious or unconscious, explicit or implicit, is basic to the development of a design for a program of teacher education. During the second half of the 1960s there was considerable activity in these areas. A number of model programs for teacher education were developed and published.

The study of teaching and teacher education was stimulated by the establishment of Research and Development Centers at Stanford University and at the University of Texas. Bush, Peck, and Roberts (1966) described the origin, functions, and promise of these institutions. Teachers' organizations were very active in the field of teacher education. In the United States, the National Commission on Teacher Education and Professional Standards of the NEA stimulated the concept of differentiated staffing through some 210 demonstration centers. Edelfeldt (1968) described these and other activities of NCTEPS. In Canada a precursor of such activity was C. E. Smith's (1962) study on *Educational Research and the Training of Teachers* commissioned by the British Columbia Teachers' Federation. Somewhat later, the Canadian Teachers' Federation published Macdonald's (1968) essays, which proposed a new emphasis in teacher education. The American Association of Colleges for Teacher Education was also active in promoting conferences and seminars. Among its many publications, *Professional Teacher Education* proposed elements for the professional sequence in teacher education (AACTE, 1968). About the same time, the AACTE-NCATE feasibility project was underway. This was a three-year study and tryout of new standards for evaluation of teacher education. Massanani's (1969) account of the procedures used in the revision of the standards describes the thorough study and involvement which occurred. As a result, a separate publication, *Standards and Evaluative Criteria for the Accreditation of Teacher Education* (hereafter called simply the *Standards*) was widely circulated (AACTE, 1967). This document lists twenty-eight standards for basic programs of teacher education, grouped under five headings: programs of instruction, faculty, students, resources and facilities, and evaluation. The NDEA National Institute for Advanced Study in Teaching Disadvantaged Youth established in 1966 culminated its activities with the publication of B. O. Smith's (1969) plan for teacher education.

Perhaps the major tour-de-force was the United States Office of Education funding of model teacher education programs. Nine were funded for Phase I (programs) and an additional one for Phase II (feasibility studies). These ten model teacher education programs, which run to over two million words, were a major contribution to the area. A general description and impressionistic evaluation is provided by Clarke (1969). Engbretson (1969) analyzed the seventy-one proposals which were not funded. His analysis is a valuable contribution to the thinking on teacher education. Throughout this paper the term *models* will denote these model programs and page or chapter references will refer to the original versions submitted to the United States Office of Education.

The paper will undertake a review and analysis of the designs and programs for the preparation of teachers published in the last half of the 1960s as described above. In addition, it will review previous studies, indicate needed research, and the requirements for such research.

DESIGNS FOR THE PREPARATION OF TEACHERS

An analysis of the elements found in the various designs for and programs of teacher education cited previously is a formidable task. Teaching is a complex activity, and teacher education is likely to be even more complex. It has a time sequence, is a process, has a structure and organization, is set in a context, and so on. The design elements abstracted by one student from so vast and complex an activity might differ from those of another. This tends to cast doubt on the objectivity of the exercise. Despite these difficulties, an analysis of the necessary elements found in the various designs and programs mentioned may be of value, and is presented below.

Factors in teaching, and in teacher education, occur in a time sequence and have degrees of proximity to the actual task. Logically and psychologically some elements in the preparation of teachers precede others. Some are remote from teaching, in the sense that there are many intervening variables, while others are close. Mitzel (1960) dealt with teaching in terms of presage, process, and product factors. Applying this terminology to teacher education, it is proposed to deal with presage factors or decisions which must be made before developing a program of teacher education, process factors or the treatments proposed, and product factors or the actual behavior produced.

Presage Factors

1. CONTEXT This refers to the anticipated future state of the world, the nation, education, teaching, and the teaching profession. The preparation of teachers is performed for such a context. Decisions about the context for which teachers are being prepared must be made in advance of planning a program of teacher education. Most of the model teacher education programs reviewed here dealt with this factor. For example, the model teacher education program developed by the Florida State University under the Phase I grants previously mentioned (Sowards, 1968) states that "the rationale for this program is based upon predictions of what society and education will be like by 1978, inferences about the nature of teaching and the role of the elementary school teacher by 1978, and implications for the preparation of elementary school teachers" (p. 3).

A number of the models, particularly Georgia (Johnson, Shearron, and Stauffer, 1968), anticipated a differentiated teaching staff and developed their programs in this context. The Toledo Model (Dickson, 1968) anticipated the demise of the self-contained classroom and developed its proposal in anticipation of the multiunit school and the concept of research and instruction units. The Pittsburgh Model (Southworth, 1968) specified that "this is a training model for individualized instruction" (p. 2). The context for *Teachers for the Real World* (Smith, 1969) was disadvantaged children, but the design boldly took the position that "this book outlines a plan for the education of the nation's teachers" (p. ix).

The fundamental issue involved in context can be handled as described above by anticipating the future and preparing teachers for this context, or by pinning one's hopes on the self-corrective devices of cybernation.

2. CYBERNATION Self-correcting devices can be located in the program or in the candidates. In the first instance, a program might be designed to produce graduates who would fit education as it is anticipated to be a decade ahead. If education were static, no change in the program would be required. Its design would remain suitable for producing graduates who would fit education as anticipated a decade ahead. On the other hand, if education were dynamic, then continual revision of the program would be required to maintain the ten-year lead. Built-in mechanisms in the design, for periodically examining and updating the program, would be cybernetic program devices. Most of the teacher education programs professed to contain just such features.

The alternate self-corrective device might be some characteristic produced in candidates. Thus, the Teachers' College Model (Joyce, 1968) proposed to produce teachers who were sensitive and flexible. Presumably, teachers with these characteristics would modify teaching in the future insofar as it was modifiable, and beyond that adapt to its changes. Thus they would fit teaching to the changed and changing circumstances of the learner of the future. On a broader level, the program proposed to develop teachers who were institution builders, interactive teachers, innovators, and scholars. Such people would modify education in the future and adapt to its changes.

A similar position was taken in the Syracuse Model:

> We assume, therefore, an uncertain future in which there will be children to educate. We further assume that since we do not know what form or how the children of such a society should be educated, . . . teachers educated today must be educated to be continually self-renewing as they adapt to and play a major role in shaping the changes that seem certain in the future world of education [Hough, 1968, p. 2].

The model proposed not only that the product be self-renewing, but that the program be self-renewing and the teacher educators be self-renewing. Hence, it combined both aspects of cybernation.

3. EXTENT OF LEAD None of the teacher education designs and programs developed during the last half of the 1960s proposed to prepare teachers for education as it is. All looked to the future—but to varying extents. In its simplest form, extent of lead refers to a one-year, five-year, ten-year, or a longer look into the future. However, it is more complex than that. It is possible to conceive of a completely objective prediction of future trends on the one hand, and a Utopian statement of what ought to be on the other. While it is difficult if not impossible to sort out the admixture, hortatory language makes one suspect an emphasis toward the Utopian. The extent of lead is the gap between what exists and the state of affairs for which teachers are being produced. For example, the Syracuse Model (Hough, 1968) speaks of "A Model program that is an open system, a program which will nurture a pluralistic and changing teacher education program in the near and somewhat distant future" (p. 2). Another example which illustrates the extent of lead is the Teachers' College Model (Joyce, 1968) statement (under the heading "Considerations for a Rationale") that "the first consideration is that teacher education must be rooted in a commitment to educational change" (p. 8). Each teacher education program explicitly or implicitly took a position on extent of lead.

4. CONTROL The question of "who decides what" cropped up in all of the models in one form or another. The right of the student to be heard was most clearly expressed in the Northwest Regional Laboratory proposal that

students and staff bargain to agreement about performance criteria (Schalock, 1698). The right of school systems to a voice in the practicum was developed in the Syracuse proposal for proto-cooperation (Hough, 1968). In outlining the essential functions of the teaching profession, Smith's *Teachers for the Real World* (1969) lists, as the very first function, education for the profession, and after developing the meaning of this function, observed that "such a concept required a new emphasis on the interrelationships between the professional personnel in teacher education institutions and in the schools" (p. 141). Perhaps because the Models funded by the United States Office of Education were prepared in such haste, there seemed to be a general tendency for the representatives of the institutions which prepare teachers to determine context, cybernation, and lead, while at the same time professing the need for the involvement of many organizations, institutions, and agencies. The following observation about the seventy-one unfunded proposals applies equally well to those funded:

> There was common agreement in these proposals that many agencies needed to be involved in planning teacher education programs, not just the College of Education. The agencies most frequently mentioned were Community and Social Agencies, State Departments of Public Instruction, the Regional Educational Research Laboratories, Psychological Clinics, Academic Departments representing those academic areas taught in the public schools, et cetera. Parenthetically it must be noted that most proposals did not reflect this agreement in the preparation of the proposals themselves [Engbretson, 1969, p. 209].

In the light of current teacher militancy, there was a strange lack of mention in the Models of participation by professional organizations. The need for such involvement was noted at a Stanford conference on the Models (May 1969) by two participants, Horton Southworth of Pittsburgh and Robert Houston of Michigan State.

The matter of control has far-reaching implications and can affect the location of teacher education (wholly in an institution, wholly in school systems, varying mixtures). Control is exercised by legislatures via certification and by university requirements via degrees. Pressures for a voice in decisions come from many groups, the most insistent of which has lately been the students themselves. Although "who decides what" is of great importance, and as such is a presage factor, it may be largely beyond the control of individuals or groups who design programs of teacher education.

5. BOUNDARIES A Teacher Education Program can be viewed as the professional preparation of teachers, while the subject matter and general education portions are regarded as "givens." It can be viewed as that which takes place in a preparing institution, or a part of a recruitment-selection-

admission-institutional preparation-internship-continuing professional education continuum. It can be viewed as preparation for what teachers do directly to mediate student learning, or it can include this plus leadership and professional activities. To clarify what is included, the boundaries ought to be specified.

The *Standards and Evaluative Criteria of Teacher Education* takes this view about general education (AACTE, 1967):

> The view reflected in the standard is that general education should include the studies most widely generalizable to life and further learning. . . . Far more important than the specific content of general education is that it be taught with generalizability rather than with academic specialization as a primary objective. . . . The professional part of the curriculum designed to prepare teachers is to be distinguished from the general studies component: the latter includes whatever instruction is deemed desirable for all educated human beings, regardless of their vocation. . . . The general studies component for prospective teachers requires that from one-third to one-half time be devoted to studies in the symbolics of information, basic physical and behavioral sciences, and humanities [p. 12].

This statement of boundaries is clear and unequivocal: general studies are part of teacher education, and in terms of time, constitute one-third to one-half. A useful distinction between general education and professional education is provided.

> The professional component covers all requirements that are justified by the work of the specific vocation of teaching. In the standards that follow . . . it is assumed, therefore, that whether a study is to be called general education or professional education does not depend on the name of the study or the department in which the instruction is offered; it depends rather on the function the study is to perform viz. whether it is to be part of general education or of specialized vocational preparation [p. 12].

With these distinctions in mind, the *Standards* call for "content to be taught to pupils, and supplementary knowledge from the subject matter field(s) to be taught, and from allied fields that are needed by the teacher for perspective and flexibility in teaching" (p. 13).

B. Othanel Smith's analysis of the problem is similar in that it recognizes general education, disciplines contributing to the teaching field, and subject matter to be taught, but adds another element: knowledge about knowledge:

> To sum up, the subject matter preparation of the teacher should consist of two interrelated parts: first, command of the content of the disciplines constituting his teaching field and of the subject matter to be taught; and second, command of knowledge about knowledge [Smith, 1969, p. 113].

Smith elaborates the second part of the subject matter preparation of teachers, knowledge about knowledge, as follows:

> The subject matter of each field of teaching is a mixture of different forms of knowledge. All of the fields contain concepts. Some contain laws or law-like statements. Others contain rules and theorems. And still others contain values either as major emphasis or as incidental to other forms of content. It is important for the teacher to be aware of these knowledge forms because studies have shown that each is taught and learned in a different way. Current programs of subject matter preparation do not enable a teacher to identify the forms of subject matter or to relate teaching behavior appropriately to the ways they are most easily learned [p. 127].

There is agreement here that general education, subject matter to be taught to pupils, and command of related disciplines are within the boundaries of teacher education. In the past, half to three-quarters of the time devoted to preparing teaching has been used on these parts. The common complaint is that the content and treatment are too frequently designed to prepare the student for further study of the disciplines. How did the Model Teacher Education Programs funded by the United States Office of Education deal with this important matter of boundaries?

The outstanding example is the Michigan State Model. The five major areas of this program are: general liberal education, scholarly modes of knowledge, professional use of knowledge, human learning, and clinical studies. The vehicle for influencing the part not directly controlled by the College of Education was involvement:

> The development of a program model such as that outlined above requires the resources of an extensive professional team. Theoretical constructs must be translated into working models and explicit instructional packages and patterns. More than 150 professional people contributed their time, effort, and expertise to the development of this model.
>
> This proposal and its implementation is the product of an effort made by seven colleges in Michigan State University: The College of Arts and Letters, Communication Arts, Social Science, Natural Science, Home Economics, Education, and the University College.
>
> Teams of educationists and scholars in the natural sciences, social sciences, and humanities worked closely together to integrate the program. While the product of their work is extremely important, the dialogue established between professional educationalists and academic disciplinarians is even more significant. Interest far beyond that required by their formal commitments was exhibited by team members through their work [Houston, 1968].

Not only was the program developed by an interdisciplinary team, but its continued direction was to be representative of the various interests. The procedure has been summarized as follows:

> An extensive and flexible management system is necessary since this program was planned and will be implemented by faculty members from seven colleges plus representatives from the public schools, preschool agencies, and students. *An Educational Policies Council* including the deans of the seven cooperating colleges will assume overall institutional responsibility for general administration of the program. A *Project Advisory Committee* with members appointed by the deans and representing the seven colleges will form a liaison agency between the Educational Policies Council and the administrative staff of the program [Le Baron, 1969, p. 91].

No other model had such a complete treatment of relationship with general education and academic disciplines. The Florida plan mentions general education, which would occupy two-thirds of the first two years, with an academic concentration in the next two years. The program recognizes the existence of these components of teacher education, but then concentrates on improvement of the professional portion. The Georgia Model is similar, but goes further in specifying approximately 25 percent of time on general education and 30 percent on an area of concentration, and in specifying that the dean of the college of education head a committee representative of all colleges responsible for the education of teachers, plus representatives from districts and the state department of education. The ComField Model of the Northwest Regional Laboratory consortium was designed to fit into the requirements for general education and a major prescribed by individual institutions. The Pittsburgh Model called for involvement of liberal arts programs in developing concepts, principles, the history of the field, the modes of inquiry, and interdisciplinary relationships.

> A two-way conversation between an academic department and the education faculty is essential to restructuring. The authors of this model have personally experienced the agonies of this confrontation. It will not be a set of easy tasks, but if teacher education is to be revolutionalized it must occur. In a general sense, these partnerships are confronted with two tasks. The first regards restructuring the knowledge system.
>
> The faculty members must examine their instructional modes. The new program will represent both a more acceptable consideration of the knowledge system and methods which are consistent with the principles of individualized instruction [Southworth, 1968, p. 50].

The Model proposed, but did not detail, linkages with the liberal arts faculties.

The Syracuse Model (Hough, 1968) has *liberal education* as one component of seven which constitute teacher education. It proposes three interdisciplinary courses designed to apply liberal arts to teacher education, each with a six-semester weight, and a policy board representative of the faculty of the disciplines involved, administrators from the colleges involved, and a student. The Syracuse Model stresses a special kind of cooperative relationship which is called *proto-cooperation,* and specifically mentions the training divisions of universities. The Toledo Model (Dickson, 1968) omitted a consideration of general education because the request for proposals did not include it.

The Wisconsin Model (Vere De Vault, 1969) makes the logical claim that teacher education is properly the responsibility of the total institution, and then goes on to describe the machinery whereby the general education, subject matter, and related disciplines can be integrated into a program of teacher education. Le Baron's summary is excellent:

> The University of Wisconsin maintains a pattern of organization for its School of Education that automatically involves all who help to prepare teachers in the making of policies for teacher education. Under this plan the School of Education functions as the overall administrative organization, a type of holding company, to marshal the total resources of the university to educate teachers and to provide research and services to schools. Wide participation in policy making is encouraged and provided, and all departments affected by policies for teacher education are expected to participate in their formulation. This all-institution approach to teacher education makes available the total university resources and facilities for a complete and systematic approach to the preparation of elementary school teachers [Le Baron, 1969, p. 184].

In his analysis of the proposals which were not funded, Engbretson (1969) observes that although the guidelines called for a statement of the relationships between the professional sequence and the entire undergraduate program, "not much detailed attention was given to these interrelationships in most of the proposals" (p. 68). He further observed that only twenty-nine of seventy-eight proposals dealt in any detail with subject matter specialization in the academic field. Involvement of persons from the academic disciplines in the preparation of the proposals was limited to twenty-seven of the seventy-eight proposals, and that number includes very minimal involvement.

The conclusion is inescapable: considerably less than half of the designs or proposals for the preparation of teachers reviewed include serious consideration of the integration of the general education, subject matter, and related discipline components into a total program of teacher education.

This dismal score is counterbalanced by that in the second aspect of boundaries. None of the programs planned teacher education as something whose beginning and end were in the institution.

Similarly, most of the Models and *Teachers for the Real World* saw the boundaries of teacher education going beyond preparation for instruction. The latter devotes a chapter to "Preparation in the Governance of the Profession." The Florida Model (Sowards, 1968) includes five program components, one of which is "Assuming Professional Responsibilities." Both the

Teachers' College and Michigan State Models have as goals the production of teachers who will be "responsible agents of social change," in the words of the latter Model. The Toledo Model was designed to produce teachers who would facilitate the development of multiunit schools and instructional units. The Northwest Regional Laboratory Model includes specifications for the development of seven noninstructional competencies.

6. SELECTION The population to be educated is an important prior decision in planning a program of teacher education. Because the personality of the individual is the vehicle through which his teaching behaviors are manifested, there are some individuals not fit to be teachers, in the sense that the institution does not have the competence, time, or money required to bring about the requisite personality development.

Selection is along two continua: from self to external, and from a one-point exit to many points of exit. Self-selection can be assisted by an extensive guidance service.

The Florida Model (Sowards, 1968) devotes a chapter to admission and screening. Familiar elements are included: intellectual requirements, abilities, commitment, physical and mental health. The Model accepts responsibility, as part of the process, for redirecting candidates to other roles in education. The Georgia Model (Johnson, Shearron, and Stauffer, 1968) also devotes a chapter to selection, which is fitted into the four categories of teaching personnel proposed: aide, teaching assistant, teacher with an area of competence, and a specialist. The Pittsburgh Model (Southworth, 1968) recognizes the importance of selection as follows:

> Improvement of teacher training rests heavily upon specific talents and personal qualities possessed by the student entering teaching as a career. To neglect or overlook talent and personal qualities would serve as an injustice to the student and to the investment in new models for teacher training [p. 32].

The Michigan State Model (Houston, 1968) includes a Career Decision Seminar for each student who enters the teacher education program, which will help the student answer such questions as the following. Shall I consider a career in teaching? Do I like to do what teaching demands? What age of children do I prefer to teach? Would I prefer to be a "general" teacher or a specialist?

Presage factors in the design of programs for teacher education represent decisions which are made prior to the development of a program and which shape the direction of the program.

Context, or what education is going to be like (assuming change), is such a factor. Cybernation is one way of dealing with change—either by built-in mechanisms in the program or by developed characteristics of the graduates. A program of teacher education has to look ahead at least four years (the time lapse between entering a freshman and beginning teaching) but probably more. The extent of lead in terms of time, or in terms of some ideal future state of affairs, is an important prior decision to any program of teacher education. Control of various elements, and the willingness of institutional personnel to share decisions which affect others, is a crucial matter today. The boundaries of teacher education, particularly the arrangements made to incorporate the one-half to three-quarters of the time which general education, subject matter, and related disciplines receive into a total integrated program for the preparation of teachers, is a crucial prior decision. Boundaries in terms of noninstructional tasks can receive varying emphasis. The selection of candidates is another presage factor. Decisions made about these factors determine the program which is developed.

Process Factors

The prior decisions already described will determine, at least partially, the process of teacher education. There is no clearcut dividing line between presage and process factors. The six factors previously described (context, cybernation, extent of lead, control, boundaries, and selection) generally precede process factors, but some presage factors, such as control and selection, can intrude into the process.

The process factors identified in the various programs and designs reviewed include dimensions, extent of individualization, graduated conceptualization-practice, support systems, and task-centered curriculum.

1. DIMENSIONS The units of the process of teacher education have traditionally been time (four years for a basic degree), credits (so many semester or quarter hours), and courses. In the model programs there is a distinct movement away from these dimensions toward performance modules—that is, distinguishable elements of teaching, or teaching tasks, which can be mastered in two to twenty hours of instruction-practice, and whose end product is teaching behavior. The term "performance criteria" is used to denote this end product of teaching behavior. The most completely developed example is in the Michigan State Model (Houston, 1968), in which over 2,700 modules are included. The standard format for these modules includes objectives, prerequisites, experience, setting, materials, level, hours, and evaluation. These criteria were designed for IBM card recording. Because it is typical, and because the topic Interpersonal Process Recall was a novel feature of this program, the second module (number 777) is provided as an illustration.

Objectives: Trainees will have begun to consider the kinds of interpersonal situation which are troublesome to them, the way in which they typically cope with such situations. They will have listened to their peers describing their ways of responding and so the candidate will have learned something about ways of coping other than his own.

Prequisites: This module may precede Module 776.

Experience: Trainees watch film entitled Stock—Rejection 1, Scene 1. At conclusion of scene pupils are asked by interrogator (Graduate Asst.) how the actor made them feel. After this is discussed he asks them how they typically react when they feel that way. Finally they are asked to contemplate alternative ways in which they might behave. They are then shown Stock—Rejection Passive, Scene 1, and again a discussion as above follows. This process continues until all of the first 2 scenes in each of the Stock and Vicki film series is completed and each has been discussed.

Setting: Blank

Materials: Filmed sequences of Stock and Vicki—currently available in IPR Library.

Level: All grades

General: All candidates

Hours: 4 hours—4 sessions of 1 hr. each, one week apart

Evaluation: Evaluation of this and next 4 modules can be determined subjectively and inferentially by the Assistant Professor leading each discussion. However, a more specific (though still subjective) evaluation can be made by examining the context of Module 780.

File: Emotional reaction coping behavior interpersonal self-analysis.

The Teachers' College Model did not use the module approach. Among the others, the form of the module varied but the general pattern was as illustrated.

It should be clear that modules could fit into the time-course-credit requirement of institutions or could mark an abandonment of these. Insofar as such modules in fact have been identified, the performance criteria specified, and the treatments required to develop these criterial behaviors have been developed, a great new dimension has been added to teacher education. Such modules could be used as the building blocks for courses and so fit into present dimensions, or could mark the end of courses. Since the modules depend on performance criteria, some students could master them quickly while other students might take a longer time. Hence, the previous uniform time dimension might be abandoned. Obviously, modules could be used to individualize the process of teacher education.

2. EXTENT OF INDIVIDUALIZATION At the one extreme, there could be a common program for all candidates. At the other extreme, there could be as many programs as there are candidates. Perhaps the major trend in teacher education as exemplified by the Models is individualization. The prime example is the Pittsburgh Model, which includes this statement:

> Also unique is the flexibility of the model which will permit and facilitate individual program designs for EACH trainee. . . . In relation to *mastery*, the trainee will be expected to work through an ordered set of objectives in the most effective way for him to obtain mastery of them. The degree of proficiency will determine mastery and his movement to another competency [Southworth, 1968, p. 27].

In general, individualization was provided by three program factors: (1) performance criteria for curricular modules, so that when the performance could be demonstrated the module was considered mastered; (2) extensive guidance service which proposed differential emphases for different individuals; (3) self-selection by students (not without some required modules).

The Northwest Regional Laboratory Model lists ten propositions in the conceptual framework underlying the model (Schalock, 1968). Number six is as follows:

> The instructional experiences that lead to both the development and personalization of competencies should be individualized with respect to point of entry into the curriculum, pacing, sequencing, information processing preferences, etc. [p. 6].

Most of the programs recognized the institutional barriers to individualized programs, such as time required for a degree and course or credit requirements.

3. GRADUATED CONCEPTUALIZATION-PRACTICE When Conant made his study of teacher education in the United States, the one common feature he noted was practice teaching. The proposals reviewed here stressed graduated exercises leading up to practice teaching such as simulation, analysis of teaching, tutoring, and microteaching. In some instances, the model makers would replace practice teaching by activities such as those listed. Graduated conceptualization-practice will now be illustrated for the Models.

The Florida Model (Sowards, 1968) proposes an "early awareness-involvement" in the preservice phase, which would include the following:

1. Individual counseling and planning with program faculty;
2. Small continuing seminars;
3. Videotape viewing sessions, accompanied by lecture and discussion;
4. Clinical involvement in simulated teaching situations, observations of ongoing classroom teaching, one-to-one tutorial experiences with

children, small group instructional experiences with children, and service assignments with selected community agencies [p. 47].

The other end of the program specifies an in-service phase of two years and three summers, including the following:

1. Work oriented toward practical problems in teaching which will be done during the regular school year.
2. On campus work during three summers designed to supplement and complement the already completed preservice phase of the program. The in-service phase is an essential part of the program. The model is so designed that to omit the in-service phase would jeopardize the total operation [p. 114].

The Georgia Model was based on a career development ladder, which, if followed, would of itself provide graduated experience. In addition, the average student would be required to take three six-week practical laboratory experiences which would involve children of different grade levels, ethnic backgrounds, and socioeconomic levels. An internship of ten weeks is provided near the end of the professional program. The graduated nature of the experiences is emphasized by the Model: "The professional program provides a continuous sequence of study and practical laboratory experiences through the media of proficiency modules" (Johnson, Shearron, and Stauffer, 1968). The Massachusetts Model (Southworth, 1968) provides for instructional skill development via microteaching, incorporates the idea of a career ladder, and includes a hierarchy of performance criteria: content knowledge, behavioral skills, and human relation skills. Since the student, with the aid of a faculty adviser, chooses his own set and sequence of learning experiences, the program provides for graduated and integrated "conceptualized-practice." The Michigan State Model (Houston, 1968) places considerable emphasis on the development of clinical behavior with the sequence starting during the first two years with tutorial experiences with children, continuing with a career decision seminar, analytical study of teaching using simulation and microteaching, through team teaching, internship, and teacher specialization. The Pittsburgh Model puts the matter very clearly:

> The clinical environment in teacher education serves three distinct functions: (1) a service function to the children or youth being educated, (2) a teaching function for both the student preparing to enter teaching and experienced teachers in residence for re-training, and (3) a research function to serve teacher education and the supporting school districts through directed observations, recorded data about selected human behavior, controlled development of materials, and deliberate evaluation procedures.
>
> Few adequately developed clinical environments presently exist in teacher

education. Very few feature a thematic approach whereby a university and school district, with full support from teacher organizations and Federal and State agencies, have established an individualized school setting for teacher training, curriculum refinement, materials development, systematic behavior analysis and evaluation.

The clinical settings need to accommodate all the preservice roles including observer, tutor, assistant teacher, student teacher, and intern teacher. Importantly, the in-service dimension of teacher education will receive greater priority in more visible and carefully established environments [Southworth, 1968, p. 39].

The emphasis on performance criteria and flexibility built into the Northwest Regional Laboratory Model (Schalock, 1968) preclude describing laboratory experiences in terms of time. The laboratory is regarded as the heart of the instructional program:

> The laboratory provides that the individual student will progress through instructional systems in which the criterion behaviors are appropriate practice of each significant performance of the effective instructional manager [p. 40].

In addition, the practicum, carried out in school settings with real pupils, is for an indeterminate time, since the neophyte must demonstrate teaching performance at specified criterion levels. The five-year program of the Syracuse Model (Hough, 1968) includes in the junior year simulated teaching, tutoring, and microteaching. In the fourth year additional practical experience with teaching units is provided, while the fifth year is a half-time internship arrangement. The student works at his own pace through various modules. It should be recalled that this model stresses proto-cooperation among such agencies as the university, the school system, and the "education industry." The facilities required for graduated experiences in conceptualization-practice would evolve from this. The Teachers' College Model (Joyce, 1968) eliminates "experiences which are analogous to those which usually characterize student teaching" but provides for the following:

Phase	*Type*	*Purpose*
Phase One	Experience the school	A four- to eight-week apprenticeship to a public school.
Phase Two	Small-Group and tutorial teaching (preferably in candidate-operated program)	Ten to twenty weeks of experimenting with teaching strategies.
Phase Three	Unit experimentation in inquiry school	Group experiments in teaching units taking four to eight weeks.

Phase	*Type*	*Purpose*
Phase Four	Experience in curriculum modes in inquiry school	Observation-participation experience in a variety of ways of teaching.
Phase Five	Carrying on an educational program	Inquiry groups develop and carry on a Candidate-Operated School Program.
Phase Six	Internship	Paid Teaching, preferably in teams derived from Inquiry Groups.

The contact laboratory begins in the first weeks of the program and continues, ideally, into the first year of paid teaching [p. 18].

The Toledo Model (1968) puts the matter this way:

> The experiences for the various target populations as reflected in the specifications require a better operational marriage between academic-cognitive type experiences than has generally been true in the past. The participation of students in actual school experience has been markedly increased over what is generally found in present programs. Much of this is related to the actual preparation for teaching in the multiunit school [p. 205].

The Wisconsin Model stresses cooperation with the schools at the preservice and in-service stages, and modules which may use various media, clinical, and laboratory experiences.

Student teaching as usually conceived is not the vehicle for graduated practice chosen by the model makers. Tutoring, simulation, microteaching, and analysis of teaching are stressed, along with a variety of internship and in-service provisions. However, there is no doubt that graduated conceptualization-practice is a prominent feature of the model teacher education programs of the late 1960s.

4. SUPPORT SYSTEMS The Models vary greatly in their treatment of management systems. Obviously, the more individualization in terms of modules which are completed when performance criteria are reached, and the more graduated conceptualization-practice experiences, the more difficult it is to keep track of the student's progress through the program. The Florida Model devotes a chapter to a computerized management control system. The Massachusetts Model has chapters on "Systems Conceptualization of the Model" and "Evaluation." The Michigan State Model, as already mentioned, developed over 2,700 modules adapted to computer storage and print out, and has a long chapter devoted to evaluation, program development, and management. The Northwest Regional Laboratory Model went further, and has

one part out of three on specifications for a system to manage the program. The Syracuse Model has chapters on the program support system, the information and evaluation support system, and the organizational support system. The Toledo Model has a chapter on evaluation. The Wisconsin Model is contained in four volumes, one of which deals with space, related educational facilities, and faculty.

Some Models used a systems analysis approach, while others avoided this, perhaps because the precision and objectivity of outcomes are inadequate, or perhaps because a systems approach seems inconsistent with participants deciding (at least in part) what happens to them. Nevertheless, there are a number of flow charts, replete with triangles and boxes, in the Models.

While some regard such support systems as a dehumanizing aspect of teacher education, nevertheless, the Models face up to the problems of recording and student accounting created by modules, individualization, graduated conceptualization-practice, and the multiple entrances and exits provided for selection.

5. TASK-CENTERED CURRICULUM The heart of teacher education is the program of experiences designed for teacher candidates. In the sources reviewed there was an emphasis on task analysis, task specification, required behaviors, treatments designed to develop these behaviors, and assessment of results in terms of the original task analysis. It will be possible to outline only the main features of curriculum.

The AACTE *Standards* (1967) previously mentioned specify curriculum factors. *The Professional Studies Component* consists of (1) content for the field of specialization; (2) humanistic and behavioral studies; (3) educational theory with laboratory and clinical experience; and (4) practice. The section on the *Faculty* refers to (1) size and quality; (2) preparation; (3) load; (4) part-time faculty; and (5) involvement with schools. The *Resources* section includes (1) library; (2) materials and instructional media center; (3) physical facilities; (4) utilization of diverse institutional resources; and (5) clerical and supporting services.

The curriculum for the preservice professional content in *Professional Teacher Education* (AACTE, 1968) covers five areas: (1) analytical study of teaching; (2) structures and uses of knowledge; (3) concepts of human development and learning; (4) designs for teaching-learning; and (5) demonstration and evaluation of teaching competencies. The suggested content in each area is research-based (e.g., Smith and Ennis, *Language and Concepts in Education;* Amidon and Flanders, *The Role of the Teacher in the Classroom;* Bellack, *The Language of the Classroom;* Hickey and Newton, *The Logical Basis of Teaching*) or theory-based (e.g., Bruner, *Some Theorems on Instruction Illustrated with Reference to Mathematics;* Bloom, *Taxonomy of Educational Objectives*). Over thirty sources such as these are cited.

Teachers for the Real World (Smith, 1969) incorporates a program of teacher education which is presented in terms of the steps required for its development.

1. *Analyze the job of teaching into the tasks that must be performed.*

   Guidelines for choosing schemes of analysis:

   a. Start with the simple—e.g., type of question, demonstrations, direct and indirect discourse.
   b. Move to more sophisticated analyses which involve the structure of teaching behavior.
   c. Categories of analysis should represent an appropriate balance among affective, cognitive, social, and psychomotor aspects of teaching.

2. *Specify the abilities required for the performance of these tasks,* e.g.:

   Minimal abilities a program of teacher education should develop are ability to:

   a. Perform stimulant operations (question, structure, probe);
   b. Manipulate different kinds of knowledge;
   c. Perform reinforcement operations;
   d. Negotiate interpersonal relations;
   e. Diagnose student needs and learning difficulties;
   f. Communicate and empathize with students, parents, and others;
   g. Perform in and with small and large groups;
   h. Utilize technological equipment;
   i. Evaluate student achievement;
   j. Judge appropriateness of instructional materials.

3. *Clearly describe the skills or techniques through which the abilities are expressed.*

4. *Work out in detail training situations and exercises for the development of each skill.*

5. *Classify training situations and exercises by tasks, abilities, skills, grade level, fields of instruction, and backgrounds of children.*

   [The reason for this indexing is that Smith perceives elements 1–4, but particularly 4, as being beyond the resources of any one institution. He advocates a series of regional, federally supported centers to work on such tasks.]

6. *Establish training complexes.*

   These are new institutions, perhaps a bit like a research and development center for teacher education, but also in charge of the practicum.

The nine Model programs originally funded for Phase I, plus the Wisconsin Model funded for Phase II, include well over two million words. Each Model is unique. Each was developed by a team of scholars. It is no easy task to delineate curricular patterns.

Following the steps described by Smith, the Model makers analyzed the job of teaching, specified the abilities, described the skills, and worked out the training situations.

The Models started with the first step: analyzing the job of teaching. Thus the Florida Model (Sowards, 1968) specified five categories of teacher behavior: formulating objectives, selecting and organizing content, employing appropriate strategies, evaluating learning outcomes, plus accepting leadership and professional responsibilities. The Georgia Model (Johnson, Shearron and Stauffer, 1968) states the matter succinctly:

> GEM's [Georgia Elementary Model] position is that the teacher education program should be designed in relation to the job the teacher is required to perform in the classroom. By defining what the job actually is, the competencies necessary to perform specific tasks may be adequately determined. In other words, it would logically follow that the content of a teacher education program should be based on the teaching act itself.

In practice, the objectives of the elementary school, plus general instructional principles, teaching principles, learning principles, and organizational principles were analyzed to educe the teaching tasks and necessary competencies. Most of the Model is devoted to this analysis of education. The Massachusetts Model (Allen and Cooper, 1968) accepts performance criteria.

> The formulation of performance criteria requires the specification of instructional and program goals in terms of behaviors to be exhibited by the trainee when instruction has been completed. . . . Careful formulation of performance criteria liberates the planners from describing the program in terms of traditional "courses" [p. 17].

As was common for other Models, the performance criteria were grouped: cornerstone criteria (human relations and behavioral), content criteria (aesthetics, language arts, social studies, science, mathematics, foreign languages, preschool), and service criteria (evaluation skills, media, and supervision). These criteria have a familiar ring. The Michigan State Model (Houston, 1968) starts from the clinical behavior style of teachers, including (1) the reflecting phase: (a) describing, (b) analyzing; (2) the proposing phase: (a) hypothesizing, (b) prescribing; (3) the doing phase: (a) treating, (b) seeking evidence on consequences. This paper has already cited one module from the Michigan State Model with its performance criteria, and has indicated the five groupings of modules: general-liberal education, scholarly modes of knowledge, professional use of knowledge, human learning, and clinical studies. The Pittsburgh Model (Southworth, 1968) lists and amplifies nine teacher competencies for individualizing instruction:

1. Specifying learning goals;
2. Assessing pupil achievement of learning goals;
3. Diagnosing learner characteristics;
4. Planning long-term and short-term learning programs with pupils;
5. Guiding pupils in their learning tasks;
6. Directing off-task pupil behavior;
7. Evaluating the learner;
8. Employing teamwork with colleagues;
9. Enhancing development [p. 13].

The Northwest Regional Laboratory Model (Schalock, 1968) lists ten items in the conceptual framework underlying the Model, which again reiterate Smith's (1969) steps previously cited. The first three follow:

1. The objectives of a teacher education program should be specified in terms of the competencies needed by teachers to bring about the outcome desired in pupils.
2. Overt behavior acceptable as evidence of given teaching competencies should be specified.
3. System design principles should be used in the development of instructional experiences to bring about the mastery of teaching competencies [p. 6].

The Syracuse Model (Hough, 1968) relates performance criteria to personal development.

> The path that has been chosen for reaching these higher level objectives of behaving and becoming, is to specify personal and professional objectives for the student at the behavioral level. The essence of these higher level objectives is incorporated into the program at the instructional level; *first,* as operational objectives; *second,* in instructional situations; and *third,* as the criteria for the assessment of student performance. The model program specifies its objectives in behavioral terms, provides situations where those behaviors can be learned, and when behaviors are manifest, assesses their quality and character in behavioral terms [p. 11].

The Teachers College Model (Joyce, 1968) proposes the categories of performance criteria previously mentioned (institution builder, interactive teacher, innovator, scholar) but avoids the detailed breakdown into numerous performance criteria and modules. The Toledo Model (Dickson, 1968) states and analyzes goals of education, provides position papers on five primary contexts through which the goals operate (instructional organization, educational technology, learning-teaching process, societal factors, and research), and then develops 818 educational specifications such as "given the instruction to describe the relation between language skills and pupils behavior, the student will write an appropriate statement" (p. 45). Each specification includes (1) behavioral objectives, (2) treatment, (3) materials, and (4) evaluation. The Wisconsin Model uses the terminology *elements* and *subelements* for the larger units of organization, and recognizes the importance of objectives, but tends to concentrate on the operations to be performed to reach the objectives. The objectives and operations are tied together.

The major features of the curriculum of teacher education were derived by analyzing the job of teaching, specifying the abilities and skills required to perform teaching tasks, developing in detail treatments which were intended to develop said abilities and skills, and arranging for graduated performance of the tasks.

Product Factors

A design for a program of teacher education will include, either explicitly or implicitly, presage factors. Six have been identified: context, cybernation, lead, control, boundaries, and selection. The programs developed by the sources reviewed exemplified five major factors: individualization, modules, graduated conceptualization-practice, support systems, and task-centered curriculum. We turn now to the product. Were the teacher candidates in fact able to do what the designs called for? If so, were they in fact able to perform as desired in the world of work?

We may note in passing that up to a decade ago, culminating in Ryans' (1960) monumental work, these questions would have been posed as follows: Were the teachers in fact what the designs called for? Was this the kind of teacher desired in the field?

Because the various sources reviewed, particularly the Models, were proposals for teacher education programs and not programs in being, these questions had to be rephrased. What provisions were incorporated to determine whether the teacher candidates could perform according to criteria, and to determine whether these criteria should be altered, in the light of performance in the field?

The AACTE *Standards* (1967) call for institutional research.

> In addition, the institution periodically will engage in research on its own program to ascertain whether its present practices are the most effective means for accomplishing its purposes [p. 16].

The emphasis here is on the product at the preservice stage of teacher preparation. Throughout the *Standards,* there is emphasis on evidence which can be used to evaluate the process.

> No institution takes its commitment to prepare teachers seriously unless it tries to arrive at an honest evaluation of the quality of its graduates and those persons being recommended for professional certification. . . . It is recognized that the present means for making such evaluations are inadequate, and that there is an emerging interest on the part of institutions in the development of more adequate means. It is assumed in the standard not only that institutions should be evaluating the teachers it has prepared with the best means now available, but also that they should be developing improved means to make such evaluations [p. 22].

Following this introduction there are three applicable standards:

> 5.1. The institution has evidence of the quality of the teachers it has prepared.
> 5.2. The institution uses the results obtained from evaluating the teachers it has prepared in the study, development and improvement of its teacher education program.
> 5.3. The institution has a long-range plan for its development and incorporates therein a plan for the development of its teacher education program [p. 22].

Teachers for the Real World (Smith, 1969) concentrates on the elements of the process, and does not stress evaluation either of the process or of success in the field. What of the Models? According to Engbretson (1969), three out of nine program components set forth in the USOE request specifically stressed this matter:

> 7. Evaluation and feedback techniques to be used throughout and at the end of the program to determine to what extent trainees have acquired the essential teaching behaviors; follow-up studies of program graduates.
> 8. Multipurpose management and evaluation system, with data storage and rapid retrieval capabilities, to permit continuous diagnosis of student progress and frequent restructuring of the trainee's learning experiences.
> 9. Plan for continually and systematically assessing, revising, and updating the program [Appendix D].

The model makers were certainly urged to take this matter into account. In his summary, Engbretson observes that the guidelines called for evaluation and feedback to determine whether the trainees had in fact acquired the essential teaching behaviors, and concludes as follows:

> Forty-seven of the 78 proposals specified some kind of evaluation or feedback mechanism or techniques while twenty-nine of the 78 specified some kind of follow-up study of graduates. In general this program component was not dealt with in great specificity among the majority of the proposals [p. 70].

Engbretson's last comment applies also to the Models which were funded. Despite the fact that both computerized management systems and curricular modules with performance criteria would facilitate institutional (process) evaluation and research, these elements were not developed in detail. The most notable exception is the Toledo Model (Dickson, 1968) which includes a position paper by Donald M. Medley who emphasizes the difference between preservice (process) and in-service (product) evaluation.

> Nowhere is it more important to maintain the distinction between teacher behavior and teacher effectiveness than when considering the problem of evaluation. The ultimate objective of any teacher education program must be to produce effective teachers, and must therefore be measured in terms of what happens to pupils. The intermediate goal of any teacher education program must be to produce teachers with certain characteristics, and must be measured in terms of what teachers do. When we wish to evaluate a *program,* then, we must confront the question, how effective are its graduates in the classroom? When we wish to evaluate a *student,* we must ask, what effect is our program having on his behavior? [p. 116].

The paper from which this was quoted also outlines research procedures for teacher education. The Model stresses the need for evaluation.

> Education today is suffering because of a lack of systematic evaluation in teacher education. It is one thing to plan a course of training for teachers but it is quite another thing to forecast how future teachers will behave once they take full responsibility for their own classrooms [p. 209].

It again reemphasizes the importance of the matter in the summary:

> There are many innovative features in the specifications for a new teacher education program. Among these none is so important as the evaluative process. For the first time in history a program has been arranged in behavioral terms so that it may not only be evaluated at a given point in time, but also so that it is self-correcting. Provisions for prompt and objective feedback are the most innovative elements and will enable all concerned to discuss the success or failure of a program to prepare educators in meaningful terms.

> This enables the implementing institutions to enter into the new program with confidence that if the selected specifications are not complete or not relevant, they will be supplemented or modified *in the regular course of the program* [p. 242].

The Model then proposes generalized steps which can be used in evaluating, and presents two fold-out diagrams of evaluation models entitled "CIPP" (Context-input-process-product) and "Hammond-Stuffelbeam Evaluation Model." According to the Toledo Model, generalized steps may be applied to four types of educational decisions: planning, structuring, implementing, and recycling. There is a kind of evaluation for each type of decision: context evaluation provides information for structuring decisions, process evaluation provides information for implementing decisions, and product evaluation provides information for recycling decisions. The Model indicates that the structure of evaluation design is the same for context, input, process, or product evaluation and identifies the major components as follows:

Focusing the Evaluation

1. Identify the major level(s) of decision-making to be served, e.g., local, state and national.
2. For each level of decision-making, project the decision situations to be served and describe each one in terms of its locus, focus, timing, and composition of alternatives.
3. Define criteria for each decision situation by specifying variables for measurement and standards for use in the judgment of alternatives.
4. Define policies within which the evaluation must operate.

Collection of Information

1. Specify the source of the information to be collected.
2. Specify the instruments and methods for collecting information.
3. Specify the sampling procedure to be employed.
4. Specify the conditions and schedule for information collection.

Organization of Information

1. Specify a format for the information which is to be collected.
2. Specify a means for coding, organizing, storing, and retrieving information.

Analysis of Information

1. Specify the analytical procedures to be employed.
2. Specify a means for performing the analysis.

Reporting of Information

1. Define the audiences for the evaluation reports.
2. Specify means for providing information to the audiences.

3. Specify the format for evaluation reports and/or reporting sessions.
4. Schedule the reporting of information.

Administration of the Evaluation

1. Summarize the evaluation schedule.
2. Define staff and resource requirements and plans for meeting these requirements.
3. Specify means for meeting policy requirements for conduct of the evaluation.
4. Evaluate the potential of the evaluation design for providing information which is valid, reliable, credible, and timely.
5. Specify and schedule means for periodic updating of the design.
6. Provide a budget for the total evaluation program [p. 217].

The Syracuse Model (Hough, 1968) recognized the importance of evaluation and analyzed the task as follows:

> *The Infomation and Evaluation Support System* is charged with four primary roles. The first is gathering data on student performance and feeding this data back to the instructional staff. Such data is essential for the self-pacing of student instruction. Secondly, the modules must be evaluated in terms of worth (both inter- and intra-module) as well as examined for the effect of differential instructional patterns. A third function of this support system would be that of analyzing the effectiveness of components and the total program. By taking into consideration outside conditions or stimuli, the program would continuously meet the divergent needs of the participants, thus insuring the continued smooth and *effective* operation of the system [p. 27].

The Model accepts Scriven's (1967) distinction between summative evaluation of developed or completed programs and formative evaluation of developing programs, and finds that the latter is applicable. It then accepts Mitzel's (1960) stages for evaluating teacher effectiveness—presage, process, and product—and describes appropriate evaluation techniques. However, it focuses on formative evaluation, and therefore tends not to stress the evaluation of teachers in service.

The Northwest Regional Laboratory Model (Schalock, 1968) poses the problem very well, but deals only very generally with procedures.

> The evaluation function involves the gathering of data to satisfy questions of how effective and appropriate the outputs of Comfield [Competency Field-centered Teacher Education Program] are as well as the impact that they make. As used here, effectiveness is concerned with determining how well Comfield accomplishes the purpose for which it was created; appro-

priateness is concerned with determining whether the objectives of Comfield are valid, that is, whether they are serving the needs for which they were established; and impact is concerned with estimating the effects of Comfield on the larger environment in which it exists. Parallel examples would be: "Can those trained in the program demonstrate the behaviors for which the training was intended?"; "Can teachers so trained deal effectively with the realities of the environment within which they act?"; and "What are the effects of Comfield on other teacher training institutions or public school graduates as they go on into high school? [p. 120].

The Michigan State Model (Houston, 1968) has a detailed list of the activities of its proposed evaluation subsystem:

1. Developing a new assessment and appraisal techniques.
2. Assisting in continuous objective development through counsel on the capacity to evaluate developed behavioral objectives.
3. Collaborating with ancillary research resources to improve design techniques.
4. Evaluating the achievement of stated subsystem objectives.
5. Designing data gathering instruments for recording student input characteristics and output behaviors.
6. Developing, with Management-Planning and Information Retrieval Subsystems, means for transmitting findings from one program or subsystem into the recycling plans of other programs and subsystems.
7. Designing means for gathering baseline data.
8. Designing systems for the collection and display of longitudinal data.
9. Recommending to the Planning Board new thrusts in research.
10. Designing means to assess the explicit behaviors as well as the attitudes and values of students.
11. Providing descriptive and research data on such persons with BSTEP as:

    a. the trainee,
    b. the on-campus faculty,
    c. the clinical professor,
    d. local school district personnel,
    e. pupils taught by the trainee, and

12. Evaluating the effectiveness of instructional modules, of all kinds, in meeting stated objectives.

The models varied in the extent to which carefully designed evaluation procedures were to be applied to the process, and in general did not deal with the much more difficult question of how well the product was performing in the field.

The reader will note that a distinction has been made between evaluation and feedback on the process of teacher education (the preservice phase) and evaluation and feedback from the product of teacher education (the in-service phase). As Medley notes, the former calls for appraisal of what changes have been made and what changes still need to be made in the individual candidate's behavior, while the latter calls for an appraisal of the program in the light of candidates' performance in the field. The *Standards* recognize the importance of such evaluation. The call for proposals issued by the USOE devoted one third of the items on program components to this matter. Despite this emphasis, there were few well-developed designs for evaluation in the Models. Perhaps because they were designs for teacher education programs, rather than descriptions of programs in being, the Models tended to stress formative evaluation.

REVIEW OF PREVIOUS STUDIES

The fourth edition of the *Encyclopedia of Educational Research* contains articles which bear on research in teacher education up to the mid-1960s. Stiles and Parker (1969), in an article entitled "Teacher Education Programs," review previous studies in terms of general theory and rationale of program conceptualization, content and design of preservice programs, clinical experiences, evaluation of teacher education programs, and promising research designs. These authors describe the situation in the past in doleful terms, but look forward to better things to come:

> Teacher education programs have been studied more than researched. Innovations have tended to be implanted and imitated with a minimum of evaluation. Practices and procedures have evolved rather than developed through controlled experimentation. . . . The past decade has seen programs of teacher education the center of intense controversy; the prospects are that this will become a field of more concentrated and more objective research in the years ahead [p. 1414].

The hope expressed in the last sentence quoted may indeed be borne out by the programs developed during the last half of the 1960s. The conceptual basis, the clearly stated objectives, the possibility of studying parts as well as wholes, the built-in evaluation devices previously cited, all contribute to the optimism expressed by Stiles and Parker.

In another article from the same source, Flanders (1969), in dealing with "Teacher Effectiveness," reviews studies to the mid-1960s, some of which bear on research in teacher education. For example, the article deals with research which links teaching processes and product; with research linking presage to process variables—e.g., in-service or preservice training and teaching behavior; and with research on presage, setting, and product variables. Flanders again sounds a note of hope for the future.

> Teacher effectiveness is an area of research which is concerned with relationships between the characteristics of teachers, teaching acts, and their effects on the educational outcomes of classroom teaching. The research which is reviewed herein permits cautious optimism and indicates that the tools long needed for the analysis of teaching-learning process are gradually being developed [p. 1423].

Insofar as research on teacher effectiveness is successful, it can be related back to teacher education. The research design, the instruments for measurement, the conceptualization of the process, and the replicable findings all feed back into and support research in teacher education.

The *Encyclopedia of Educational Research* also includes articles by Davies and Amershek (1969) on "Student Teaching," by Gage (1969) on "Teaching Methods," and by Biddle (1969) on "Teacher Roles." Much of the research reviewed has implications, even if not direct, for research in teacher education.

The second *Handbook of Research on Teaching* soon should be available. This, with the original *Handbook* (Gage, 1963), will provide a review of related research.

The regular reviews of research on various topics which appear in the *Review of Educational Research* include an article in the June 1967 issue by Denemark and Macdonald (1967) on the topic of preservice and in-service education of teachers. This review of the subject to the mid-1960s generally agrees with the preceding analyses.

> Although the general or liberal arts aspects of the education of teachers are said to be crucial for the program, no direct research on general education as it relates to teacher education was located by the reviewers. . . .
>
> Research on the role of the disciplines, per se, was equally disappointing. . . .
>
> After student teaching, the most frequently studied area of teacher education was instructional methods and media. . . .
>
> It is apparent from a review of the literature that the large grants for teacher education have been given for program development and not for theory development or research activity . . . [pp. 235–41].

A review of trends in teacher education programs, which provides a good description of the changes in emphasis in the various elements of programs, is provided by Harap (1967).

In the 1968 issue of the *International Review of Education,* A. Yates, the editor, notes these trends: a shared concern about the quality and quantity of recruits; a dissatisfaction with arrangements for professional education of teachers; a need for close links between the university, teacher education programs, and the schools; and an awareness that teachers can no longer be considered potentially capable of performing all tasks. In the same volume, Cogan (1968) has this to say about teacher education in the United States:

> There is a scarcity of plans aimed at fundamental reconstruction of teacher education. This is in part a consequence of the complexity and scope of the unknowns built into the problem. . . . It appears likely that reforms in teacher education will follow rather than precede new conceptualizations of education itself [p. 394].

The most recent study which reviews research on teacher education is in a special area but is notable for an excellent bibliography of ninety-five items. The study, by Blosser and Howe (1969), appeared in *Science Teacher* and summarizes trends as follows:

> Since 1964 there has been an increase in the amount of research on programs for educating science teachers. Such studies still, however, are few in number. Most of the investigations have focused on verbal interaction analyses, microteaching situations, simulation techniques, and general outcomes of teacher education programs [p. 91].

In summarizing the research on teacher education to the mid-1960s, one could state that the area was active rather than dormant. The large grants were for program development rather than for research. Even so, there was a dearth of proposals for the fundamental reconstruction of teacher education. However, the interest and activity described paved the way for a more optimistic view of the future.

The review of research provided by this author will not include the important but detailed studies on interaction analysis, microteaching, and simulation techniques. Seven articles on research in student teaching were found: Garland, Williams, and Corrigan (1968), McLarin (1968), Yee (1968), Sorensen (1967), Dumas (1966), Hinely, Galloway, Coody, and Sandefur (1966), and Popham (1965). These covered such diverse topics as developing an instrument for measuring role expectations for student teaching, relating student teaching marks to personality variables, developing and testing a triad model for interpersonal relationships, teaching styles, and effects of methods courses on performance. Even more studies of attitudes were found: studies of attitudes of different kinds of candidates (elementary vs. secondary, various majors), changes in attitude, the effect of teacher candidates' attitudes on performance, and the like. The authors were Giebink (1967), Brim (1966), Chabassol (1968), Walberg, Melzner, Todd, and Henry (1968),

Horowitz (1968), Davis and Yamamoto (1968, 1969), McAulay (1968), Jacobs (1968), Miller (1968), and Wagoner and O'Hanlon (1967). Five studies were found (although there must be many more) dealing with personality. McCaw (1967) found that teachers in training did not in fact hold ideas directly contradictory to the personality dimension *authoritarianism*. Seibel (1967) showed that using personality measures it was possible to predict teaching behavior. Amidon (1967) reported a 2½-year study on the effect upon the behavior and attitudes of both student teachers and cooperating teachers of training in interaction analyses. A major finding was that such training increases student teacher indirectness. Kosier and Vere De Vault (1967) found that college instructional approaches had some effect on personality traits. Joyce, Dirr, and Hunt (1969) reported an experiment of the pretest-treatment-posttest type where interpersonal sensitivity was tested and sensitivity training was the treatment. The context was teaching. Some indirect changes were found rather than those that were hypothesized.

Two good articles on theory development were found. Joyce and Hodges (1969) present an excellent review of efforts to develop theoretical concepts to guide teacher education during the first half of the 1960s, and list five areas of reality around which the components of their proposed rationale were built: education decision-making, control over teaching styles, control over the analysis of teaching, control over research skills through the research component, and control over self. Spodek (1969) dealt with a model for a teacher education program in early childhood education by identifying six assumptions and dividing the content of the program into preactive, interactive, and proactive stages (the latter being evaluation and feedback), and listing and describing six components of teacher education: selection and recruitment, general education, professional foundations, instructional knowledge, practice, evaluation and program modification.

Research turned up only one experimental study which compared two different programs of teacher education. Sandefur *et al.* (1967) compared the behavior of fifty students in a program of teacher education for secondary school teaching with sixty-two in an experimental program, where the latter stressed coordination of laboratory experiences with conceptualization. The experimental group was rated as demonstrating more desirable teaching behaviors.

Two survey-type studies of the product in the field were noted. Beaty (1969) reported on all the 1964 graduates of one Tennessee teacher education institution three years later, half of whom were teaching in the state. Practically all of those who had prepared for teaching in the elementary school and who were then in teaching were employed in elementary schools, but nearly seven out of eight of social studies (secondary) majors were misplaced. Beaty concluded that most of the complaints about the professional sequence were related to misplacement. He further concluded as follows:

> An institutional follow-up study can provide a teacher education institution a valuable source of information both in assessing the opinions of the graduates of its training program and in providing leads for program improvement [p. 302].

Jay (1968) reported that certificated graduates are polled each year. He too reports misplacement. Slightly over one-third of the graduates secured positions in their own state. Open-ended comments on their preparation elicited the following lists of their "felt needs":

> More practical experience, more observation, more in the area of discipline, more on professional organizations, additional preparation in subject matter other than the major field, and too much theory [p. 23].

The reviews of research cited agree that there has been considerable activity in teacher education concentrating on implementing new programs. But there was a dearth of theory, a dearth of revolutionary new proposals for teacher education programs, and no research on programs as such. Despite these deficiencies, reviewers in the mid-1960s were optimistic about future trends. Since that time there have been numerous studies on microteaching, interaction analysis, and simulation not reviewed here. These studies, along with detailed and particularistic studies of student teaching, attitudes, and personality are developing an accretion of specific knowledge about teacher education. In addition, in the late 1960s one finds a few articles on the conceptual framework of teacher education and on product evaluation.

A giant step forward, however, is the designs for teacher education programs described in the first part of this article.

PROSPECTS FOR RESEARCH ON TEACHER EDUCATION PROGRAMS

It is a truism that research should be guided by theoretical frameworks. The process of teaching is complex. The program of teacher education is likely to be even more complex. A sound conceptual framework capable of both analyzing and synthesizing is required. The Models described in the first part of this paper have developed such theoretical framework, no doubt influenced by the USOE guidelines.

Research on teacher education programs can be micro research or macro research. The latter could be on large groupings of elements such as the previously cited categories of the teaching task developed by the Florida Model: formulating objectives, selecting and organizing content, employing appropriate strategies, evaluating learning outcomes, and accepting leadership and professional responsibilities. Macro research could also be on still larger groupings generally termed teaching style. The magnitude of macro research will probably mean that much micro research, on the units or elements of programs, will precede. Here the Models have made a tremendous contribution through the development of hundreds and even thousands of modules. One can anticipate dozens of studies of the pretest-treatment–posttest-time-lapse–second-posttest type, if teacher education students are streaming through modules, each of which requires, say, four hours. Such studies may well develop instrumentation useful for further research in teacher education. One can also anticipate studies of the type where high performers on a given module and low performers on the same module teach pupils whose gains in some characteristic are compared (with no significant difference!). There may be studies of the time taken to master a module to criterion, related to variables such as the candidate's personality, attitudes, or even to student performance.

It may be that these are unfounded anticipations. There are 1,200 institutions preparing teachers in the United States, one hundred in Canada, and so on for other countries, and only ten Model programs. The reader may make his own forecasts about dissemination. The point is that Models which can be disseminated have been developed.

The reader will recall that Smith (1969) advocated a series of regional, federally supported centers to work on the tasks of analyzing teaching, specifying abilities, describing skills or techniques, and working out training materials for teacher education. If such curricular materials are developed, standardized "treatments" can be plugged into micro research. This would promote replicability of studies.

Macro research on the teacher education process can go hand in hand with carefully formulated evaluation procedures. The major components of evaluation design previously cited for the Toledo Model could provide the data which could be used to test hypotheses, to compare the products of different institutions, to relate differences found in various factors, and the like. Such studies constitute research on total programs of the kind mentioned by Turner in the previous chapter: theory-multiunit research-argument about causality. This reviewer sees the trend of events, strongly reinforced by the Model Teacher Education Programs, as being favorable for micro and macro research on teacher education programs.

Research on product, or how teachers actually behave in the field, is another matter. Years ago, George S. Counts wrote a book entitled *Dare the Schools Build a New Social Order?* Applying this question to the Models one can paraphrase Counts and ask "Dare the Teacher Education Institutions Create a New Education?" On reading the Models, one is aware that some model builders would answer the paraphrased question with a ringing "yes." Product research might then be based not on how well the candidates teach in the field, but on how well the candidates proceed to revolutionize the field.

This same difficulty can occur in a less generalized form. If the candidates are prepared for education in the future involving a differentiated staff, or team teaching, or individualized instruction (of a particular type), or the like, but if on entering teaching they find the customary self-contained classroom at the elementary level or subject departmentalization at the secondary level, how then is product research to proceed? Does it accept the situation and determine how well the candidates are performing in the field as it is, or does it accept the candidates' preparation and condemn the field for not being different? *Context, cybernation,* and *lead* decisions previously mentioned are crucial.

The obvious solution to the problem involved in the choice between a generalized rebuilding of education or particularized changes such as "differentiated staff" is the *proto-cooperation* advocated so capably in the Syracuse Model. Presumably, when the school systems which receive teachers, the institution which prepares them, the government agencies which regulate certification, elements of curriculum, and the like, and other education agencies are generally agreed on *context, cybernation,* and *lead,* then product research would be simplified. However, there would still be problems. The two surveys of teaching which were cited (and which represent a kind of research which is extensively performed and seldom published) find migration and misplacement among graduates. If education in the field is reasonably uniform from state to state, province to province, country to country, then migration does not present a problem. One suspects that while there is great uniformity there may be some diversity. Is education in the United States the same as in Canada, or in Maine the same as in California? The reader will recall that about 50 percent of the teachers prepared as reported in one study, and just over one third in the other, were teaching in their home state. Turning now to misplacement, one can ponder how one does research if the "product" was prepared to teach social studies but in fact is teaching, say, mathematics.

Another real problem about product research is that the pressure to use it locally, and not to publish so that it enters the mainstream of research reporting, is very great. If the findings show that the products of the institution seem to be satisfactory in a number of ways, it is argued that no one else would be interested, while if they are unsatisfactory, it is argued that the institution ought not to be publicly embarrassed. A major deleterious effect of unpublished product research is that the instrumentation and procedures are not available to assist other researchers or for review of their adequacy.

An additional problem about product research is what group might best do it. Typically, professors are expected to do research and are rewarded for it. However, they are part of the institution which may be evaluated as a result of the research, and the teachers providing the information may not communicate as freely as they would to more neutral researchers. The school systems have a difficulty: their teachers come from many sources. Product research done by a school system might provide valuable comparisons. However, there is little motivation for school systems to do such research. How would they use it? State education departments could do it with the advantage of neutrality. Teachers' organizations are perhaps in the best position, and have one of the largest stakes in doing such research or sponsoring it. It can be expected in the future that more and more product research on teacher education will be done by or sponsored by teachers' organizations. Probably it will be published only in local channels, but certainly it will form the basis for local discussions, hopefully, of the *proto-cooperation* type.

It would be impossible to more than mention the procedures required for product research. The *Fourth Encyclopedia of Educational Research* has an excellent article by Herriott (1969) on "Survey Research Method." Normally, a questionnaire is involved. Careful preparation, editing, jury-of-expert review, pilot study, tests of reliability of item, and interview validation are required for sound survey research. Open-end items, such as incomplete sentence items, may improve the validity of the data collected even as they increase the difficulty of analysis. The reader is again referred to the Toledo Model treatment of evaluation previously cited.

The prospects are bright for continued micro research in teacher education. The invention of interaction analysis, micro teaching, and simulation exercises has promoted such research. Lazarsfeld is said to have remarked that when man invented the hammer, everything had to be hammered. Micro research needs more hammers, and perhaps one in sight is the curricular material mentioned by Smith. Certainly, the modules developed by the Model builders should promote micro research.

Macro research is more complex, but the theoretical underpinning is rapidly being developed, and the inclination to attempt such research seems to be on the increase. Substantial grants from such sources as the Federal Government or foundations will be needed to support the large-scale effort required.

Despite all the difficulties, product research is likely to continue, and to continue to remain largely unpublished. One can only hope that, working in the dark, the various researchers will use defensible survey research methods.

SUMMARY

In the latter half of the 1960s there were a number of major publications which delineated programs of teacher education: AACTE *Standards* (1967), AACTE *Professional Teacher Education* (1968), Smith's *Teachers for the Real World* (1969), and ten model teacher education programs funded by the United States Office of Education. An analysis of these sources reveals presage, process, and product factors in the program designs.

Six presage factors, or decisions which precede the design of a program of teacher education, were identified. *Context* refers to the anticipated future state of the world, nation, education, teaching, and hence the context in which teacher education is set. *Cybernation* refers to self-corrective devices in the program, or in characteristics produced in the candidates, which tend to retain congruence in changing circumstances. *Extent of lead* refers to the gap between what exists and what is forecast, or between what exists and what it is deemed ought to exist, or some combination of these. *Control* is simply "who decides what." *Boundaries* refers to the domain of teacher education, particularly whether such matters as general education and subject matter preparation are included, whether teacher education is solely that which occurs within an institutional setting, and whether nonteaching tasks are included in the preparation of teachers. *Selection* can be along two continua: self to external, and one gate to many gates. These six factors are called *presage* because decisions about them are required before planning a program of teacher education.

There is no clearcut dividing line between presage and process factors. In the programs reviewed process factors included *dimensions, extent of individualization, graduated conceptualization-practice, support systems,* and *task-centered curriculum.*

The common *dimension* was a small curricular unit called a module, featuring performance criteria, limited time requirements, and specified materials and treatments designed to produce the criterial performances. All of the models reviewed proposed increased *individualization* of program based on the curricular modules just mentioned, extensive guidance services, and self-selection of program components. *Graduated conceptualization-practice* was provided by simulation exercises, analysis of teaching, tutoring, micro teaching, and the like. Most of the model programs of teacher education recognized that if modules were used, if programs were individualized, and if a number of entrance and exit points were provided for selection, then computerized student accounting *support systems* were required. Perhaps the most important feature of the programs of teacher education reviewed was their derivation from analyses of the task of teaching. The term *task-centered curriculum* was used to denote this task analysis, task specification, statement of required teaching behaviors, specification of materials and treatments, and assessment of results in terms of the task analysis.

The product factors, or teacher behaviors to be produced, were specified in many of the sources reviewed. Designs to evaluate these behaviors were not, on the whole, well-developed, with the exception of one model teacher education program. Evaluation and feedback on the process of teacher education call for an appraisal of what changes have been made and what changes still need to be made in the individual candidate's behavior, while evaluation and feedback on the product call for corresponding activities in the light of the candidate's performance in the field.

A review of previous studies of research on teacher education showed cautious optimism commencing in the mid 1960s, and considerable activity of the micro research type in such areas as student teaching, attitudes, and personality. Only one or two articles on theory development or on evaluating a program of teacher education were found, except in the Models reviewed.

The prospects for research on teacher education programs are bright. The Models have provided considerable development of theory. Modules lend themselves to micro research. There is a ferment of activity in teacher education. The most difficult area is research on the total program in terms of success in the field. It is suspected that studies of this nature often remain unpublished.

REFERENCES

Allen, D. W., and J. M. Cooper, 1968. *Model Elementary Teacher Education Program.* Washington, D.C.: USOE Bureau of Research, U.S. Government Printing Office, FS 5.258:58022.

American Association of Colleges for Teacher Education, 1967. *Standards and Evaluative Criteria for the Accreditation of Teacher Education: A Draft of the Proposed New Standards, with Study Guide.* Washington, D.C.: AACTE.

———, 1968. *Professional Teacher Education: A Program Design Developed by the AACTE Teacher Education & Media Project.* Washington, D.C.: AACTE.

Amidon, E., 1967. *The Effect upon the Behavior and Attitudes of Student Teachers of Training Cooperating Teachers and Student Teachers in the Use of Interaction Analysis as a Classroom Observational Technique.* Philadelphia: College of Education, Temple University.

Beaty, E., 1969. "Follow-up of Teacher Education Graduates as a Basis for Institutional Improvement." *Peabody Journal of Education,* 46:298–302.

Blosser, E., and R. W. Howe, 1969. "An Analysis of Research Related to the Education of Secondary School Science Teachers." *Science Teacher,* 36:87–95.

Brim, B. J., 1966. "Attitude Change in Teacher Education Students." *Journal of Educational Research,* 59:441–45.

Bush, R. N., R. F. Peck, and C. Roberts, 1966. "Research, Development and Innovation in Teacher Education." *American Association of Colleges of Teacher Education Yearbook,* 19:120–27.

Chabassol, D. J., 1968. "The Possession of Certain Attitudes as Predictors in Practice Teaching." *Journal of Educational Research,* 61:304–6.

Clarke, S. C. T., 1969. "The Story of Elementary Teacher Education Models." *Journal of Teacher Education,* 20:283–93.

Cogan, M. L., 1968. "Patterns in the Education of Teachers in U.S.A." *International Review of Education,* 14: No. 4 (special number).

Davis, O. L., and K. Yamamoto, 1968 and 1969. "Teachers in Preparation: I. Motivation, Identional Fluency and Interprofessional Attitude." *Journal of Teacher Education,* 17:205–9; "Teachers in Preparation: II. Professional Attitudes and Motivations." *Journal of Teacher Education,* 19:365–69.

Denemark, G. W., and J. B. Macdonald, 1967. "Preservice and Inservice Education of Teachers." *Review of Educational Research,* 37:233–47.

Dickson, G. E., 1968. *Educational Specifications for a Comprehensive Elementary Teacher Education Program.* Washington, D.C.: USOE Bureau of Research, U.S. Government Printing Office, OE-58023.

Dumas, William Wayne, 1966. "Strengths and Weaknesses of Student Teachers in English." *Journal of Experimental Education,* 35:19–27.

Edelfeldt, R. A., 1968. "The Implications of Differential Utilization of Personnel for Preparation Programs." *American Association of Colleges for Teacher Education Yearbook.* Washington, D.C.: AACTE.

Engbretson, W. E., 1969. *Analysis and Evaluation of Plans for Comprehensive Elementary Teacher Education Models.* Final Report, Project No. 8–8056, Grant No. OEG-0-8-08805644 (010). Washington, D.C.: U.S. Department of Health, Education, and Welfare, Office of Education, Bureau of Research.

Flanders, N. A., 1969. "Teacher Effectiveness." *Encyclopedia of Educational Research,* 4th ed. New York: The Macmillan Company.

Gage, N. L., ed., 1963. *Handbook of Research on Teaching.* Chicago: Rand McNally and Co.

Garland, G., C. Williams, and D. Corrigan, 1968. "Procedures for Developing and Validation of a Role Expectation Instrument for Student Teaching." *Journal of Teacher Education,* 19:25–32.

Giebink, J. W., 1967. "A Failure of the MTAL to Relate to Teacher Behavior." *Journal of Teacher Education,* 18:233–39.

Harap, H., 1967. "A Review of Recent Developments in Teacher Education." *Journal of Teacher Education,* 18:15–19.

Herriott, R. E., 1969. "Survey Research Method." *Encyclopedia of Educational Research,* 4th ed. New York: The Macmillan Company.

Hinely, R. T., C. M. Galloway, B. E. Coody, and W. S. Sandefur, 1966. "An Exploratory Study of Teaching Styles among Student Teachers." *Journal of Experimental Education,* 35:30–35.

Horowitz, M., 1968. "Student Teaching Experiences and Attitudes of Student Teachers." *Journal of Teacher Education,* 19:317–24.

Hough, J., 1968. *Specifications for a Comprehensive Undergraduate and Inservice Teacher Education Program for Elementary Teachers.* Washington, D.C.: USOE Bureau of Research, U.S. Government Printing Office, FS5.258:58016.

Houston, W. R., 1968. *Behavioral Science Elementary Teacher Education Pro-*

gram. Washington, D.C.: USOE Bureau of Research, U.S. Government Printing Office, FS5.258:58024.

Jacobs, E. B., 1968. "Attitude Change in Teacher Education: An Inquiry into the Role of Attitudes in Changing Teacher Behavior." *Journal of Teacher Education,* 19:410–15.

Jay, R. H., 1968. "Follow-up Study of First Year Teachers." *Montana Education,* 45:23–24.

Johnson, C. E., G. F. Shearron, and A. J. Stauffer, 1968. *Georgia Educational Model Specifications for the Preparation of Elementary Teachers.* Washington, D.C.: USOE Bureau of Research, U.S. Government Printing Office, FS5.258:58019.

Joyce, B. R., 1968. *The Teacher Innovator: A Program to Prepare Teachers.* Washington, D.C.: USOE Bureau of Research, U.S. Government Printing Office, FS5.258:58021.

Joyce, B., P. Dirr, and D. E. Hunt, 1969. "Sensitivity Training for Teachers: An Experiment." *Journal of Teacher Education,* 20:75–83.

Joyce, B., and R. E. Hodges, 1966. "A Rationale for Teacher Education." *Elementary School Journal,* 66:254–56.

Kosier, K. O., and M. Vere De Vault, 1967. "Differentiated Effects of Three College Instructional Approaches on Personality Traits of Beginning Elementary Teachers." *Journal of Experimental Education,* 35:19–27.

Le Baron, W., 1969. *Analytical Summaries of Specifications for Model Teacher Education Programs.* Washington, D.C.: USOE Bureau of Research.

Macdonald, J., 1968. *The Discernible Teacher: Three Essays on Teacher Education.* Ottawa: Canadian Teachers' Federation.

McAulay, J. D., 1968. "Social Political Attitudes of Elementary Teachers." *Journal of Teacher Education,* 19:405–9.

McCaw, W. R., 1967. "Cognitive Dissonance and Teachers-in-Training." *Journal of Experimental Education,* 35:50–52.

McLarin, E. W., 1968. "Sixteen P.F. Scores and Success in Student Teaching." *Journal of Teacher Education,* 19:25–32.

Massanari, K., 1969. "The AACTE-NCATE Feasibility Project: A Test of Proposed New Accreditation Standards for Teacher Education." *Journal of Teacher Education,* 20:5–13.

Miller, H. L., 1968. "The Relationship of Social Class to Slum School Attitudes among Education Students in an Urban College." *Journal of Teacher Education,* 19:416–24.

Mitzel, H. E., 1960. "Teacher Effectiveness." *Encyclopedia of Educational Research,* 3rd ed. New York: The Macmillan Company.

Popham, W. J., 1965. "Student Teachers' Classroom Performance and Recency of Instructional Methods Coursework." *Journal of Experimental Education,* 34:85–88.

Ryans, D. G., 1960. *Characteristics of Teachers.* Washington, D.C.: American Council on Education.

Sandefur, J. T., *et al.,* 1967. *An Experimental Study of Professional Education for Secondary Teachers.* Washington, D.C.: USOE Report No. CRP-2879.

Schalock, H. D., 1968. *A Competency Based, Field Centered, Systems Approach to Elementary Teacher Education.* Washington, D.C.: USOE Bureau of Research, U.S. Government Printing Office, FS5.258:58020.

Scriven, M., 1967. "The Methodology of Evaluation." *Perspectives of Curriculum Evaluation.* AERA Monograph Series on Curriculum Evaluation. Chicago: Rand McNally and Co.

Seibel, D., 1967. "Predicting the Classroom Behavior of Teachers." *Journal of Experimental Education,* 36:26–32.

Smith, B. O., 1969. *Teachers for the Real World.* Washington, D.C.: American Association of Colleges for Teacher Education.

Smith, C. E., 1962. *Educational Research and the Training of Teachers.* Vancouver, B.C.: British Columbia Teachers' Federation.

Sorensen, G., 1967. "What Is Learned in Practice Teaching?" *Journal of Teacher Education,* 18:173–78.

Southworth, H. C., 1968. *A Model of Teacher Training for the Individualization of Instruction.* Washington, D.C.: USOE Bureau of Research, U.S. Government Printing Office, FS5.258:58017.

Sowards, J. W., 1968. *A Model for the Preparation of Elementary School Teachers.* Washington, D.C.: USOE Bureau of Research, U.S. Government Printing Office, FS5.258:58018.

Spodek, B., 1969. "Constructing a Model for a Teacher Education Program in Early Childhood Education." *Contemporary Education,* 40:145–49.

Stiles, L. J., and R. P. Parker, 1969. "Teacher Education Programs." *Encyclopedia of Educational Research,* 4th ed. New York: The Macmillan Company.

Vere De Vault, M., 1969. *Wisconsin Elementary Teacher Education Project.* Madison: School of Education, University of Wisconsin.

Wagoner, R. L., and J. P. O'Hanlon, 1967. "Teacher Attitude toward Evaluation." *Journal of Teacher Education,* 19:471–75.

Walberg, H. J., S. Melzner, R. M. Todd, and P. M. Henry, 1968. "Effects of Tutoring and Practice Teaching on Self-Concept and Attitudes in Education Students." *Journal of Teacher Education,* 19:283–91.

Yee, A. H., 1968. "Interpersonal Relationships in the Student Teaching Triad." *Journal of Teacher Education,* 19:95–112.

Name Index

Subject Index